access to history

THE UNIFICATION
OF ITALY
1815–70

access to history

THE UNIFICATION OF ITALY 1815–70

Second Edition

Andrina Stiles

Hodder & Stoughton
A MEMBER OF THE HODDER HEADLINE GROUP

Acknowledgements

The front cover illustration shows a portrait of Garibaldi by Filippo Palizzi, reproduced courtesy of Museo del Risorgimento/Photo Scala.

The publishers would like to thank the following for permission to reproduce material in this book: Cambridge University Press for extracts from *Society and Politics in the Age of the Risorgimento: Essays in Honour of Denis Mack Smith*, 1991, by John Davis and Paul Ginsborg; Picador for extracts from *The Kidnapping of Edgar Mortara* by David Keltzer, 1997.

The publishers would like to thank the following for permission to reproduce copyright illustrations in this book: AKG London pages 22, 61; theartarchive page 20; The British Library page 23; Foto Scala, Firenze pages 18, 62 (bottom), 65; Index, Firenze page 62 (top); *Les Souverains venus à Paris en 1867 pour l'exposition* by Charles Porion, ©Photo RMN – Château de Compiègne page 83.

Every effort has been made to trace and acknowledge ownership of copyright. The publishers will be glad to make arrangements with any copyright holders with whom it has not been possible to contact.

Orders: please contact Bookpoint Ltd, 78 Milton Park, Abingdon, Oxon OX14 4TD. Telephone: (44) 01235 827720, Fax: (44) 01235 400454. Lines are open from 9.00–6.00, Monday to Saturday, with a 24 hour message answering service. Email address: orders@bookpoint.co.uk

British Library Cataloguing in Publication Data
A catalogue record for this title is available from The British Library

ISBN 0 340 75386 2

First published 2001
Impression number   10 9 8 7 6 5 4 3 2 1
Year   2005 2004 2003 2002 2001

Typeset by Fakenham Photosetting Ltd, Fakenham, Norfolk, NR21 8NN
Printed in Great Britain for Hodder & Stoughton Educational, a division of Hodder Headline Plc, 338 Euston Road, London NW1 3BH by Redwood Books, Trowbridge, Wilts.

Contents

Preface

To the general reader

Although the *Access to History* series has been designed with the needs of students studying the subject at higher examination levels very much in mind, it also has a great deal to offer the general reader. The main body of the text (i.e. ignoring the 'Study Guides' at the ends of chapters) forms a readable and yet stimulating survey of a coherent topic as studied by historians. However, each author's aim has not merely been to provide a clear explanation of what happened in the past (to interest and inform): it has also been assumed that most readers wish to be stimulated into thinking further about the topic and to form opinions of their own about the significance of the events that are described and discussed (to be challenged). Thus, although no prior knowledge of the topic is expected on the reader's part, she or he is treated as an intelligent and thinking person throughout. The author tends to share ideas and possibilities with the reader, rather than passing on numbers of so-called 'historical truths'.

To the student reader

Although advantage has been taken of the publication of a second edition to ensure the results of recent research are reflected in the text, the main alteration from the first edition is the inclusion of new features, and the modification of existing ones, aimed at assisting you in your study of the topic at AS level, A level and Higher. Two features are designed to assist you during your first reading of a chapter. The *Points to Consider* section following each chapter title is intended to focus your attention on the main theme(s) of the chapter, and the issues box following most section headings alerts you to the question or questions to be dealt with in the section. The *Working on ...* section at the end of each chapter suggests ways of gaining maximum benefit from the chapter.

There are many ways in which the series can be used by students studying History at a higher level. It will, therefore, be worthwhile thinking about your own study strategy before you start your work on this book. Obviously, your strategy will vary depending on the aim you have in mind, and the time for study that is available to you.

If, for example, you want to acquire a general overview of the topic in the shortest possible time, the following approach will probably be the most effective:

1. Read Chapter 1. As you do so, keep in mind the issues raised in the *Points to Consider* section.

2. Read the *Points to Consider* section at the beginning of Chapter 2 and decide whether it is necessary for you to read this chapter.
3. If it is, read the chapter, stopping at each heading or sub-heading to note down the main points that have been made. Often, the best way of doing this is to answer the question(s) posed in the Key Issues boxes.
4. Repeat stage 2 (and stage 3 where appropriate) for all the other chapters.

If, however, your aim is to gain a thorough grasp of the topic, taking however much time is necessary to do so, you may benefit from carrying out the same procedure with each chapter, as follows:

1. Try to read the chapter in one sitting. As you do this, bear in mind any advice given in the *Points to Consider* section.
2. Study the flow diagram at the end of the chapter, ensuring that you understand the general 'shape' of what you have just read.
3. Read the *Working on ...* section and decide what further work you need to do on the chapter. In particularly important sections of the book, this is likely to involve reading the chapter a second time and stopping at each heading and sub-heading to think about (and probably to write a summary of) what you have just read.
4. Attempt the *Source-based questions* section. It will sometimes be sufficient to think through your answers, but additional understanding will often be gained by forcing yourself to write them down.

When you have finished the main chapters of the book, study the 'Further Reading' section and decide what additional reading (if any) you will do on the topic.

This book has been designed to help make your studies both enjoyable and successful. If you can think of ways in which this could have been done more effectively, please contact us. In the meantime, we hope that you will gain greatly from your study of History.

Keith Randell & Robert Pearce

1 Italy 1815–20 Rulers and Subjects

POINTS TO CONSIDER

After your first reading of this introductory chapter you should know what is meant by 'The Restored Monarchies' and be able to decide whether their governments were 'reactionary' or not. You should also have an opinion about whether Italians were better off under Napoleon than they were under the Restored Monarchies and if so, why?

KEY DATES

1789–1815	Napoleon's Italy.
1815	The final defeat of Napoleon and his exile to St. Helena.
	The Congress of Vienna meets and hands control of Italy to Austria.
	The 'Restored Monarchs' begin to return to their Italian states.

1 French control of Italy ends and Austria takes over

> **KEY ISSUES** Life in Napoleon's Italy – was it better or worse for Italians than under the Restored Monarchies? Do the Restored Monarchs deserve their reputation as reactionary (backward looking) rulers?

In 1815 French control of Italy came to an end with the defeat of Napoleon at Waterloo and his final exile to St. Helena and was replaced by that of Austria.

Nearly twenty years before in 1796 when Napoleon's army overran Italy the country had eleven independent states along with a number of tiny principalities. Napoleon made a series of changes which simplified political boundaries. In 1798 he did away with the old complicated pattern of states and divided most of the country into just four separate republics. In 1810 he divided the country again, but this time into three parts. One third was annexed to France and treated as part of the French Empire, another third was known as the Kingdom of Italy, and the remaining third as the Kingdom of Naples. When Sicily was added to the Kingdom of Naples the combined kingdom was often referred to as 'The Kingdom of the two Sicilies' (see map on page 93). In a somewhat similar way the northern state of Piedmont had originally been known as 'The Kingdom of Sardinia', or 'Sardinia-Piedmont', but after 1815 was referred to simply as Piedmont.

All Napoleon's boundary changes were set aside after his defeat at Waterloo and his final exile to St. Helena. The European powers meeting at the Congress of Vienna in 1815 decided to return Italian state boundaries to more or less what they had been in the middle of the eighteenth century before Napoleon's arrival and as they were to remain until the 1860s and unification. Even more importantly, the Congress decided that the best way to prevent any future threat of French invasions was to give Austria control of Italy. In the north, where French influence had been strong, Lombardy and Venetia would be governed directly from Vienna, and Tuscany and the Duchies of Modena and Parma be given new Austrian rulers. The Austrian Chancellor Metternich's plan 'to extinguish the spirit of Italian unity and ideas about constitutions' seemed to be working well. As he said at the time, 'Italian affairs do not exist'.

In 1815 the old ruling families were clamouring to be allowed to return to Italy from the exile in which most of them had lived out the Napoleonic era. They were anxious, now that their old state boundaries had been restored, to return to their previous lifestyle. It was not long before kings, princes, dukes and duchesses were finding their way back to Italy. Their return was generally welcomed by the landowning nobility of the countryside, by the well-to-do middle class in the towns and, especially, by the Pope and the Roman Catholic Church. For all these it signalled a welcome return to the old ways.

With very few exceptions the peasants, who made up about 90 per cent of the population, neither knew nor cared what was happening outside their own villages. Whether it was the French, the Austrians or a Restored Monarch who ruled was of little or no importance to them in their struggle for survival.

2 Life under French Rule

> **KEY ISSUE** What was good and what was bad about French rule of Italy?

Historians are very divided over what life had been like for the Italian people under French rule. Some believe, 'Italy's experience during the period was traumatic from every point of view' and that the 'brutality and irreligion of the French soldiery' was largely to blame. A great many men were required for the French army and a great deal of money was needed to train, equip and feed the French soldiers and the Italian conscripts. Twenty-seven thousand Italian soldiers accompanied Napoleon to Russia in 1812 and only a thousand, many of them badly wounded, survived to return home on foot, having lost in the campaign all their horses and cannon. Italians deeply resented the increased conscription of young men into the army, along with the high taxation needed to make good the loss of so many soldiers, horses and weapons. War, though, was Napoleon's life and as much as 60 per cent of tax revenue collected in Italy by the French authorities was used to fund military expenditure even in peace time.

The Roman Catholic Church was one body which had suffered severely under French rule. Its power was greatly reduced and two Popes were actually carried off to France. In 1809 the temporal power (worldly power of the Pope as ruler of the Papal States) was declared to be at an end. The Papal States were to be governed by the French instead of by the Pope and his Cardinals. This did not affect the Pope's spiritual (religious) authority for he remained head of the Church, but by 1814 almost all monasteries had been closed down by the French and the church lands sold off, not in the small lots the peasants hoped for and might have been able to buy, but in large lots to already landowning noble families or to wealthy merchants from the towns who wanted to set up as landed gentry.

Whether the families of well-to-do noble landowners and of middle-class bankers and merchants in Piedmont suffered under French rule is unclear. Accounts vary widely, but many were written as memoirs long after the events they describe and may not be entirely accurate. The families of two noblemen who later became Prime Ministers of Piedmont, Cavour and D'Azeglio are good examples. The Cavours seem to have done well out of the purchase of church lands, while D'Azeglio, in memoirs written nearly half a century later, complains that his family was ruined under French rule.

There were however substantial benefits from French rule for most of the ten per cent or so Italians who lived in towns. The majority of these were professional men and their families, well-to-do middle-class merchants, lawyers, bankers, apothecaries, doctors and government officials. Lower in the social scale tradesmen, artisans and craftsmen all profited too from the increased prosperity of the middle class as changes introduced by Napoleon brought financial and business advantage. External customs barriers were simplified and internal trade barriers between states swept away, weights and measures standardised, tax collection reorganised, new and better roads built and transport improved. French civil law (the *Code Napoleon*) was introduced nationally to replace the earlier hotchpotch of separate state laws, and new local government districts were set up along French lines. Industry was encouraged (although only for the benefit of France) and vaccination against smallpox was made available. Street lighting in towns was introduced, though there are suggestions that in Milan at least this new attempt to make the streets safer at night was not appreciated, because, 'The streets were illuminated by oil lamps, and the flickering of the flames quite blinded the pedestrians' making them even easier targets for pickpockets and other criminals.

The most important development for the future was probably the introduction by the French of a two-chamber representative government in each of the states. Many young Italian men were able to gain experience of politics and government in these 'parliaments'. Others gained experience of leadership as officers in the French army of occupation or in the conscripted, well trained Italian army of 80,000 men. These experiences were to stand both groups in good stead in the years of revolution and nationalist struggle.

3 Peasants

> **KEY ISSUE** How can the life of Italian peasants best be described in a few sentences?

Meanwhile, peasant families who made up between 80 and 90 per cent of the 18 million or so Italians in the early 1800s continued to live a life far removed from that of the elite (important and influential because wealthy and well educated) middle-class families of Piedmont or Tuscany, or the old aristocracy of southern Italy and Sicily. Italian peasant families, ignored in their life time and long dismissed by historians as uneducated, unimportant, non-political and unworthy of study are just beginning to be the focus of new research. The Italian historian Marzio Barbagli for instance, has made an intensive study of the ages at which men and women married within the peasant communities in different parts of Italy and whether they set up their own home or lived with the parents of one of them in an extended family. In the rural south of Italy couples married comparatively young, women at 19 years of age and men shortly before they were 25. They were able to do this because 'It is customary for the parents of a girl who is going to be married to supply her with a set of dowry gifts, that is a bed, some clothes and linen'. Where the families were poor this was usually impossible, so 'in the case of landless labourers, a young man will set up a household with a few pence of his own, a few from his wife and whatever he can borrow and at once start a family'. In Sardinia, because her father did not give her a dowry, a girl had to make with her own hand the things she needed to take with her. As she had very little time during the day, the work took a long while to complete and the age at which she was free to marry was higher than elsewhere. Many young men were never able to marry at all because it was customary in some areas that the head of the family must remain a bachelor. Most peasants lived as they had always done in dark, damp, poorly furnished cottages which they shared with their livestock for warmth at night. They tilled their fields with wooden ploughs, perhaps with the help of a horse, perhaps not, and carried their crops home on their backs, for over most of rural Italy a wheeled cart was unknown. Unfortunately, the most easily and therefore most commonly grown crop was maize. When eaten in large quantities as the staple diet it results in vitamin deficiency and gives rise to the terrible disease pellagra which causes madness and ends in suicide. In one year in the early nineteenth century 95,000 cases were reported among peasants in Venetia alone. Rather than remain almost permanently on the verge of starvation, the prey of bad weather and failed crops, many young men left the family farms, took to the hills and became bandits, and many young women moved into the towns looking for work where they often found instead diseases such as typhoid, cholera, diphtheria and tuberculosis spread by overcrowding with as many as 80 people in a house, a non-existent sewage system and a lack of clean drinking water. Many women in both town and country discovered, if they did manage to find a job or to obtain work which could be done at home, that it was impossible to keep their babies and often abandoned them at the nearest foundling hospital. There a rotary container set in the front door allowed a baby to be left with some sort of identification. The container could be turned round in such a way that someone inside would find, remove and, the mother hoped, care for the baby. If conditions improved the mother would return and reclaim her child at a later date, months or sometimes years later. By then the child might well be no longer alive for the death rate in foundling hospitals was high.

Peasant women, if they remained in the countryside, were expected not only to help their husbands in the fields and to feed and care for their families, but to make a little money at home as outworkers for some urban merchant by spinning or weaving, sewing shirts or, with the help of the children, raising silk worms and reeling off the silk from the resulting cocoons for the major Italian manufacturing industry of silk weaving.

4 The Restored Monarchs 1815–1849

> **KEY ISSUES** Did life for Italians change under under the Restored Monarchs? Were Italians better or worse off than under French rule? Why?

The Restored Monarchs have for long been seen by historians as trying to turn the clock back to pre-Napoleonic times in an attempt to return to absolute government. Their alliance with the Church, which was itself seen as reactionary (backward looking) and their general friendliness with the Habsburg government in Austria, has led historians to write off the Restored Monarchs as reactionary too. Between 1815 and Unification in 1859–61 the social upsets and revolutions which took place were until recently described by historians as a struggle between progress (working to make Italy a united independent nation, often through membership of secret societies) and reaction (out-of-date absolute rule, brutal oppression, and a general opposition to popular nationalist ambitions for Italian unity and independence).

New research by revisionist historians suggests a different situation. Revisionist historians are those who look at the evidence for the usually accepted explanation of a historical event and then decide whether that explanation is, in the light of new knowledge or new understanding, the best explanation of what happened, or whether another one is better. They now suggest that in only a few states and on a few occasions did Restoration governments behave in a reactionary way. Most of the opposition to these governments, revisionists say, was not because popular demands for a part in government were being ignored. The real trouble, revisionists suggest, was just the opposite. It was not because monarchs were keeping too much power in their own hands, but because they were modernising their governments and setting up a central administration to carry out everyday business. They point out that similar government changes were taking place in other European countries and that there was popular opposition there too. It is true that Restoration governments used censorship, police surveillance and military force to deal with unrest – but so did most other European states in the early nineteenth century. There was therefore nothing special about Italy as a whole compared with other countries. There were though four states for which no excuse can be found – they were indeed backward looking – Piedmont, Modena, the Papal States (Rome and the surrounding territory, ruled by the Pope) and Naples.

When King Victor Emanuel I returned to Piedmont and Duke Francesco IV to Modena in 1815 they both set out to turn the clock back to pre-Napoleonic days. Middle-class officials in the government and law courts, and non-noble officers in the army who had been appointed under Napoleon were dismissed, and replaced by members of the old noble families. In addition, the French law code was done away with and the former eighteenth century laws, with their special privileges for the nobility, were restored. In Piedmont the old customs barriers were reintroduced, the use of the new roads built by the French was actively discouraged, control of education was handed back to the Roman

Catholic Church, and the Jesuits who had been exiled by Napoleon were invited to return. Nobles were given back their lands and, at the same time, the old anti-Jewish laws restricting ownership of property were reintroduced and Jews were once again ordered to remain in the ghettos instead of being allowed to move freely about the country.

A series of hardline Popes, known collectively as 'the zealots', between them established a tight hold on government, education, culture and politics within the Papal States. All central and local government was in the hands of priests. The lay population had almost no say in what happened. Censorship was strictly imposed and all opposition forcibly repressed. Religious persecution was increased, and all toleration of any other belief than Roman Catholic doctrine was forbidden. Jews, in particular, came in for harsh treatment. Their children could be taken away to be brought up as Catholics by the Church if it could be shown or alleged that anyone – a friend, a servant, or a relative – had baptised them secretly. The seizing from his home in the ghetto of a young Jewish boy, Edgar Mortara, who may or may not have been baptised by a simpleminded servant girl, created a great sensation which helped, despite the opposition of the Pope, to bring the practice of kidnapping to an end. For a time the Papal States had the unenviable reputation of being the most backward and oppressive of all the Italian states.

In Sicily the King of Naples cancelled the constitution which had limited his power by allowing the people a say in government and which had been in use in the island since 1812. At the same time, he declared that Sicily would in future be governed as part of the kingdom of Naples. Liberals and Radicals joined together to demand a new constitution. The king refused their demand and in 1820 there began the first of a long drawn out series of revolutions which are dealt with in Chapter 2.

Napoleon had said, 'Italy is one nation. Unity of customs, language and literature must at a period more or less distant unite her inhabitants under one government, and Rome without doubt will be chosen by the Italians as their capital'.

In the early 1800s this scenario was for Italian nationalists only a dream. By the 1860s the dream had come true. How it happened is the subject of the rest of this book.

References

1   Lucy Riall, *The Italian Risorgimento* (Routledge, 1994) Chapter 2.
2   David Keltzer, *The Kidnapping of Edgar Mortara*, (Picador, 1997).
3   Italy Since 1800 (Absalom).

Summary Diagram

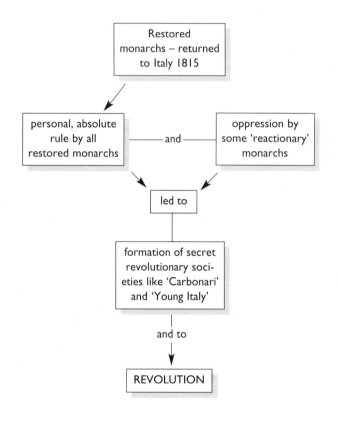

Restored
monarchs – returned
to Italy 1815

personal, absolute
rule by all
restored monarchs

— and —

oppression by
some 'reactionary'
monarchs

led to

formation of secret
revolutionary soci-
eties like 'Carbonari'
and 'Young Italy'

and to

REVOLUTION

Working on Chapter 1

This chapter should be regarded as a background or curtain-raiser to the events that led to the struggle to achieve the unification of the peoples of the various Italian states. It describes the changes brought about in the Italian peninsula during the years of French occupation (1799–1814) and the nature of the rule of the former absolute sovereigns after their restoration at the end of the Napoleonic era. Regard the chapter as an outline of these events. Although the syllabuses of examination boards tend to cover the period 1848–1870, it is very useful to have a working knowledge of the events that came before.

Answering structured questions on Chapter 1

The questions used at AS and A-level are of various types – structured questions, questions based on one, two or more sources and, of course, essay questions. Let us begin by considering structured questions. Such questions are divided into two or more sub-sections that usually increase in difficulty with the later questions requiring a greater depth of knowledge and a more in-depth approach than the first. Remember the later questions carry the highest marks! In answering such questions you will be required to recall, select and use your historical knowledge accurately and express your knowledge in a clear and effective manner.

Before attempting the following questions, read through the chapter again bearing in mind the extent of the changes brought about in the government of Italy and the status of the various classes of Italian society before and after the overthrow of Napoleon in 1815.

1. a) Explain briefly the steps taken by Napoleon I to extend French influence over the Italian states after 1799. (*8 marks*)

 b) To what extent were the Restored Monarchs able to regain their former power and status in Italy after 1815? (*12 marks*)

2. a) On page 2 what did Metternich mean when he said 'Italian affairs do not exist'? (*4 marks*)

 b) To what extent was the Papacy able to reimpose its authority on the Italian people after 1815? (*6 marks*)

 c) Do the views of modern day revisionist historians differ significantly from those held previously regarding the nature of the rule of the Restored Monarchs? Explain your answer fully. (*10 marks*)

2 Risorgimento and Revolution 1820–49

POINTS TO CONSIDER

The important topic for you to understand in your first reading of this chapter is what the revolutions were about and why they failed. Make sure you also know what each of the political groups believed and what made them different from and opposed to one another.

KEY DATES

1820–1 The first wave of revolutions broke out in Sicily, Naples and Piedmont, and were unsuccessful.

1831–3 The second wave of revolutions broke out in Modena, Parma and the Papal States and were even more unsuccessful.

1833 Mazzini founded 'Young Italy'.

1846 Pope Pius IX elected.

1848–9 The third wave of revolutions broke out in Sicily and Naples and spread quickly to Piedmont, Tuscany, Modena, Parma, Venetia and Lombardy where revolutionaries came into conflict with the Austrian army.

1849 Roman Republic established in February and overthrown in June.

1852 Cavour became Prime Minister.

1 Italian Politics in 1815

KEY ISSUE Who were the political groups and what did each believe?

There were a number of different political ideas current in Italy in 1815.

a) Liberals: Liberals believed that the people had the right to some say in government and that this was best done through a representative assembly or parliament elected by property owners. Liberals were also concerned with establishing a rule of law which guaranteed certain rights, such as a fair trial, and certain freedoms, such as free speech for all citizens. They were generally non-violent, mainly middle-class, and distrusted both absolute monarchies and republican democracies. They favoured instead constitutional monarchy, that is a king who would be bound by certain agreed restrictions on his power set out in a written document (the constitution).

b) Radicals: Radicals were much more extreme in their views. They wanted social reforms and a fairer distribution of wealth and were prepared to use violence as a way to obtain their goals. Many of them were members of revolutionary Secret Societies such as the Carbonari and believed that political power should lie with the people, not with a parliament unless it were elected by all men over the age of 25 and not just by property owners. There was of course no thought of giving a vote to women or to the peasants. Radicals had only one point of contact with Liberals – opposition to the Restored Monarchies.

c) Nationalists: Nationalists believed that people of the same race, language, culture and tradition should be united in an independent nation of their own. It should have clear geographical boundaries and not be subject to control by any other nation. Many nationalists went further and wanted a republic instead of a monarchy. Liberals and Radicals both supported nationalism and unification as the way forward for Italy, even though they did not agree on whether the means should be peaceful or violent.

d) Metternich's View: The Austrian Chancellor Metternich's approach was entirely negative. He was totally opposed to nationalism, liberalism and radicalism. He had no intention of allowing such dangerous ideas to spread and perhaps undermine Austrian control over Italy. He believed Austrian safety depended on maintaining the jigsaw of separate states ruled by absolute monarchs and was content that 'Italy' as a united nation should continue not to exist. In 1815 there were no 'Italians', only Neapolitans, Piedmontese, Tuscans and the rest and, he argued, that is how it should stay as this would keep Italy weak, divided and easily controlled by Austria.

Metternich was not alone in these beliefs. Even intelligent, well educated men saw nothing but difficulties in the way of unity between the states. The Piedmontese ambassador to Russia wrote about the possible takeover of Genoa by Piedmont:

1 '... The acquisition of Genoa will have dangers for us. The union of nations encounters no difficulties on the map, but in reality it is a different matter. There are peoples who cannot be mixed; perhaps the Piedmontese and Genoans fall into this class, separated as they are by
5 ancient and ingrained hatred. Where will the capital be? and where unity?'

In 1815 local loyalties were still more important to most Italians than dreams of national unity.

2 Secret Societies

KEY ISSUES What did the secret societies want and who belonged to them? Why were they not very successful?

In 1820, when revolutions broke out first in Sicily, then in Naples and Piedmont, secret societies played an important part. These societies are thought to have developed from eighteenth-century Freemasonry where men formed themselves into groups pledged to mutual protection with secret passwords and semi-religious rituals. The Church viewed these groups with grave suspicion as anti-Catholic and as a danger to the established social order. In the 1790s similar groups whose main purpose was to drive out the French sprang up all over Italy. After 1815 their aims changed to overthrowing the restored monarchs and to driving out the Austrians.

The societies attracted a wide variety of members, army officers, students, lawyers, teachers and doctors, all well educated and mostly middle-class. A few noblemen also joined but peasants and workers were almost unknown. The majority of members were patriotic, enthusiastic and daring; many were idealists, some were dreamers, a few were rogues and criminals, all wanted to be leaders, and all were happy to risk their lives in wild adventures and impossible missions. The great weakness of the societies was their unwillingness to act together and their lack of an overall organisation. Most societies were small and scattered. Sometimes they did work together, but much more often on their own and, because of the societies' emphasis on secrecy, historians are still not sure how successful they were.

Far and away the best known and most important of the societies was the Carbonari. The name means 'charcoal burners' and it has been suggested that the earliest members were men who sold charcoal for domestic fuel. They were particularly active in southern Italy, especially in Naples, where they are thought to have had about 60,000 members. This was probably about 5 per cent of the adult male population and the government of Naples became worried enough to order the suppression of the society. Their efforts failed and membership of the Carbonari went on rising. It is known that they had elaborate rituals and swore unquestioning obedience to their leaders. Unlike many of the other societies it was not particularly anti-Catholic, and although they planned armed revolution and the overthrow of the existing social order, they were not committed republicans. Their aims were surprisingly mild ones. In Piedmont they hoped to establish a constitutional monarchy, that is to have a king with limited power. In Naples they did not want to replace the King with a republic, but just to persuade him to grant a constitution.

3 Revolution

> **KEY ISSUE** Why did the revolutions take place? Why did they not succeed?

a) 1820–1

The 1820 revolutions began in Naples where, in 1818, King Ferdinand had greatly increased the Church's power to censor books, newspapers and magazines with which it disagreed. This angered the middle class, lawyers and teachers in particular, because freedom of speech was being made impossible. As Ferdinand was short of money he cut back on public spending, halted works like road and harbour improvements and reduced still further what little education was available to the people. Poverty, corrupt government and restrictions on personal freedom became general. So too did discontent, not just in Naples but in the other half of Ferdinand's kingdom, Sicily, which had been forcibly united with Naples. Sicilians felt Ferdinand's government was concentrating on Naples and neglecting the island's needs. Agricultural prices fell sharply and the effect on the Sicilian economy was disastrous, particularly for the peasants who found themselves getting more and more into debt.

In January 1820 news of a revolution in Spain encouraged the Liberals in Naples to take action. Led by a priest and supported by 100 non-comissioned officers and soldiers from the cavalry, 30 Carbonari members advanced on the town of Avellino and a widespread uprising soon took place. The attempt by the government troops to round up the rebels was very half-hearted, particularly after one of the commanding officers, General Pepe, led one infantry and two cavalry regiments to join the rebel army with himself at the head of what had now become a revolution. In July, King Ferdinand promised to meet the rebels' demands for a constitution within a week, but the revolutionaries did not trust him. They wanted the constitution to be like the one granted in Spain in 1812 which gave the vote to all adult males to elect a single-chamber parliament. The king agreed subject to certain possible changes at a later date and for a time it looked as if the revolution had after all been a success, especially when the revolutionaries led by General Pepe marched into the city of Naples and were received by the king. A new government was appointed, Pepe was put in charge of the army, the king swore to defend the constitution and the Carbonari gained large numbers of recruits.

While all this was going on another and separate revolt had begun in Sicily where the people were determined to fight for independence from Naples. Riots took place in Palermo, the Sicilian capital. There were demands for a constitution, government offices were burned down, prisoners released and the Neapolitan governor sent home by boat as the revolutionaries took over the city.

In Naples the first meeting of the newly elected parliament took place in October 1820. Its members were middle-class professional men, lawyers, bankers, and merchants, along with a few noblemen, some priests, but of course no peasants or women. Members discussed what had happened in Sicily and agreed that at all costs the island must remain part of the Kingdom of Naples. The island of Sicily must not be allowed to declare independence and must be brought to heel by Neapolitan armed force if necessary.

The Austrian Chancellor, Metternich, was greatly disturbed that the Neapolitan revolution had apparently been so successful. He did not approve of revolutions – they were unsettling events which disturbed the peace not only of the state in which they happened but in neighbouring states also. Therefore, he argued, it was only right for the Great Powers (Austria, Prussia and Russia) to meet and if necessary take action to suppress such disturbances wherever they occurred. In 1821 the King of Naples was invited to attend one such meeting. There he declared that he had been forced to grant the constitution out of fear and asked for Austria to help him restore his absolute rule. Metternich was delighted by this because it gave him a chance to intervene in Italy. In March 1821 the Austrian army entered the city of Naples despite a brave resistance led by General Pepe. Severe reprisals were handed out to the citizens indiscriminately by the Austrian authorities. Arrests, imprisonments and executions became so common that even Metternich was shocked by the savagery and ordered the dismissal of the chief of police.

Piedmont was the other state which saw revolution erupt in 1820. The king, Victor Emmanuel I, had pursued a very reactionary policy since his return and almost all evidence of French rule had been destroyed. Equality before the law had been abandoned and the right to a free and open trial abolished. The king also declared that the old constitution of 1770 would remain in force and could not ever be changed. Piedmont would therefore remain an absolute monarchy in spite of continued pressure by a small group of liberals.

When news of what was happening in Naples reached Piedmont discontent came out into the open. The Carbonari rapidly gained new members, and university students, army officers and liberals combined to establish a revolutionary government in the town of Alessandria where they proclaimed their independence as the 'Kingdom of Italy' and declared war on Austria. An army mutiny in Turin encouraged Victor Emmanuel I to see his situation as hopeless and to abdicate.

The Liberals now turned to the young man Charles Albert, second in line to the throne, for leadership. He issued a vague proclamation referring to the Spanish Constitution of 1812 as 'a law of state', though adding that changes might be made to it later. Victor Emmanuel's brother and first in line to the throne, Charles Felix, was temporarily absent from Piedmont, so for the time being Charles Albert took control and appointed a new government. A message speedily arrived from Charles Felix denouncing Charles Albert as a rebel and refusing to accept any change in the form of government. Charles Albert took fright and fled from Turin, leaving the city to the Liberals. They prepared to fight to defend the constitution which Charles Albert had granted, while Charles Felix appealed to

Metternich for Austrian help. This help came, and Austrian troops, together with troops loyal to Charles Felix, defeated the forces of the Turin Liberals. Hundreds of revolutionaries went into exile. The 1820–1 revolutions were over and until 1823 Piedmont was occupied by an Austrian army.

b) 1831–3

In 1830 there was a revolution in France. Italian liberals became excited by the possibility that the French would support Italian revolutions and disturbances broke out again, this time in Modena, Parma and the Papal States. In most of these places the aim was a moderate one – to persuade their ruler to grant a constitution. In Modena the revolt was led by Enrico Misley, the student son of a university professor. He trusted his own ruler, the Duke Francesco of Modena, to whom he revealed his plans for a united Italy, but his trust was betrayed and he was arrested two days before the uprising was due to begin in February 1831.

Miseley's arrest encouraged Duke Francesco to believe that the danger was over and he went to Vienna to negotiate Austrian help should it be needed on some future occasion. While he was away revolutionaries took over the city of Modena and set up a provisional government. This encouraged students in neighbouring Parma to organise riots and to demand a constitution from their ruler, the Duchess Marie-Louise. She fled in terror and a provisional government was established by the students. Contact with revolutionaries in Modena was at once made and a joint army commander appointed. The revolutionaries had little time to organise, for within a month Duke Francesco had returned to Modena at the head of troops who remained loyal to him and quickly defeated the revolutionaries. Savage reprisals were taken and anyone suspected of supporting the rebels was arrested, imprisoned, exiled or executed. Even a moustache or beard could lead to arrest as a revolutionary.

Similar uprisings took place in the Papal States, organised this time by the professional classes who resented the oppressive rule of the Church authorities. The Papal government put up little resistance and a provisional government known as 'The Government of the Italian Provinces' was formed in Bologna in February 1831. It did not last long. Austrian troops moved into the Papal States and defeated the rebels. Minor uprisings continued during 1831 and 1832 but they were fiercely suppressed by the violent and undisciplined Papal troops.

4 Revolutionary Success and Failure 1820–31

KEY ISSUE Why did the revolutions of 1820–31 fail?

The revolutions of 1820 and 1831 achieved very little. In Piedmont, Naples and the Papal States reactionary governments strengthened their hold with the help of Austria and by using military force where necessary. Naples recovered control over Sicily and made a future attempt at breaking away less likely by abolishing the trade guilds whose members had been leaders of the revolution there.

Where revolutions were successful in ousting their rulers the success was only temporary and due more to the failure of the governments to take effective action, to the rulers' habit of running away, and to the governments' lack of military resources than to the strength of the revolutionaries. Remembering what happened in the French Revolution of the end of the eighteenth century many rulers expected to be defeated. This gave the revolutionaries an early advantage, but one which they quickly lost through their failure to take united action.

The revolutions were weakened by being local affairs, concerned only with limited areas. There was little communication between the revolutionaries in the different states and even less co-operation. The revolutionary government in Bologna refused to send help to Modena. Elsewhere revolutions were not co-ordinated. They relied heavily on a network of small groups of revolutionaries set up by the Carbonari and other secret societies, but these were isolated units and their aims differed from place to place. Most revolutionaries were surprisingly moderate in their demands and not given to violence: usually all they were trying to achieve was the granting of a constitution to allow the people some part in government.

The revolutionary movements were mainly middle-class, except in Sicily where peasants were involved. Elsewhere popular interest and support was not encouraged by the revolutionary leaders. Not surprisingly, ordinary people often welcomed back their former rulers with open arms because middle-class revolutionaries did not want mass involvement in revolution. They feared that allowing a mob of less well educated people to join in the revolutions would lead to calls for a democracy which would replace parliament by what we would now call 'people power', would unsettle society and its class divisions, and would replace monarchies by republics.

5 The *Risorgimento*

> **KEY ISSUE** What was the *Risorgimento*?

The *Risorgimento* was the nationalist movement which played an important part in the unification of Italy. The word 'Risorgimento', which first came into use at the end of the eighteenth century, means 'resurgence' or 'rebirth', in this case the rebirth of Italy not as the

GIUSEPPE MAZZINI

-Profile-

1805 Born in Genoa, intelligent, sensitive, physically frail and subject to depression.

1821 Became a nationalist after seeing Piedmontese refugee revolutionaries begging in the streets.

1822–27 Studied medicine (collapsed at sight of blood) and law (became bored).

1827 Joined Carbonari, but was betrayed in 1830. While imprisoned decided he must work for the independence and unification of Italy.

1831 On his release he moved to the south of France where he founded the new secret society, 'Young Italy'.

> 1 'Young Italy' is a brotherhood of Italians who believe in a law of progress and duty and are convinced that Italy is destined to become one nation. They join with the intention of remaking Italy as one independent nation of freemen and equals... republican
> 5 government is the only form of government which ensures the future... 'Young Italy' is unitarian because without unity there is no true nation.

Believed political education and revolution essential to ultimate aim of Italy as "republic one and indivisible".

Appealed to The People for support.

1837 Went into exile in London.

1849 High point of Mazzini's life. Returned to Italy as head of Roman Republic until Rome fell to French in June 1849. Again exiled to London where he lived in poverty writing 10,000 letters and 100 books of articles. His writings very difficult to understand as political message even by educated minority. Not understood by The People. Not the way to encourage popular revolution.

1872 After 40 years in exile returned secretly to Italy. Died in Pisa and buried in Genoa his birthplace.

After death criticised by Italian newspapers as 'this dangerous enemy of free and united Italy' who had made 'frantic efforts to keep the country divided'. Outside Italy praised as 'a born leader of men' and the 'greatest, bravest, most heroic of Italians'. 1946 still being described by Italian historians as 'nothing but a terrorist' and still subject of very different verdicts by historians today.

Question: What made him so distrusted not just in his lifetime, but long after, by his own countrymen? Clue: what did he think about the Church and Christianity, the Monarchy, and The People? Read section 6 to find out.

Giuseppe Mazzini.

result of war or diplomacy, but as the final stage of a gradual transformation into a united and independent nation.

In the 1830s Giuseppe Mazzini and, for a time, Pope Pius IX took up the theme of national unity.

6 More about Mazzini

> **KEY ISSUE** Were Mazzini's ideas practicable or was he sure to fail in attracting support?

Mazzini's own political beliefs were based on the existence of God; on the equality of men and of races; on the progress of mankind, and on the rights and duties of the individual in society. In his attitude to religion, through, he was out of step with the Catholic Church. He believed Christianity was a worn out religion and needed to be replaced by something else – democracy. God was no longer speaking through the scriptures or through priests but through the People. What the people wanted was therefore the will of God, and as the people wanted national independence and unity this had to be achieved. This was why he set up 'Young Italy'.

Those who joined Young Italy had to swear to work to make Italy 'one free independent republican nation'. Monarchs who granted a constitution were only making a half-hearted move towards a republican Italy. When Charles Albert finally became king of Piedmont in 1831 Mazzini wrote to him about the coming revolution and invited him to become its leader. 'Put yourself at the head of the nation; write on your banner "Union, Liberty, Independence". Give your name to a century'. 'Not that I have any hopes of him', he said at the time and he was right. No reply came from Charles Albert which was just as well, for what would Mazzini have done, as a staunch republican opposed to monarchy, if Charles Albert had said 'Yes'?

In 1833 a Mazzini-inspired revolt took place in the Piedmontese army but was betrayed and savagely crushed by the authorities. Some other Mazzinian revolutionary activities were laughably pathetic. In 1833, for another planned attack on Piedmont, Mazzini based himself in Switzerland and began to collect Polish, German and Italian refugees as volunteers. The military command was entrusted to General Ramorino from Genoa and Mazzini gave him money to raise and organise an army. Ramorino took the money to Paris where he lost it gambling and returned to Mazzini without an army and without the money. In Switzerland all Mazzini was left with were the men whom he himself had collected together. Just before they were ready to leave for Piedmont the Swiss authorities surrounded and disbanded the Polish and German volunteers. This left fewer than two hundred men and Ramorino felt it was no good going on with such a small number. He ordered them to disperse and while he and Mazzini argued about what to do next, the soldiers obeyed their commander's orders and went home. The expedition had finished before it began.

Mazzini's dream of uniting Italy was not realised in the 1830s, although 'Young Italy' did gain an important recruit in 1833 when a young man involved himself in a proposed Mazzinian revolt in Genoa. The scheme failed but the young man escaped before his trial and was sentenced to death in his absence. He was Giuseppe Garibaldi.

Mazzini's ideas were too intellectual, too idealistic and too impractical to be a real basis for revolution. His writings were appreciated only by a small number of well-educated revolutionaries and even they did not always understand what he meant. Although Mazzini went into exile which lasted forty years, apart from short intervals when he returned secretly to Italy, he kept in close touch with what was happening there and continued his political activities from a distance. His weakness was that he failed to realise the needs of the peasants and the importance of working for reforms in the countryside, which could have won him widespread support and changed his movement from a minority one into a popular one. His spectacularly open return to become head of the Roman Republic in 1849 was probably the high point of his life.

Mazzini was not the only possible candidate for revolutionary leader. In Piedmont moderate nationalists proposed that their state should lead the other Italian states in an attempt to drive out the Austrians who were still occupying much of northern Italy. Supporters of this idea argued that only Piedmont was strong enough to reclaim Lombardy and Venetia from the Austrians. There could be no independent united Italy until this was done and it was only a

POPE PIUS IX

-Profile-

1792 Giovanni Maria Mastai-Ferretti was born in Ancona, ninth child of a noble family with strong church connections. Not academically gifted. Destined for army career.
1807 Developed epilepsy, so entered church instead.
1819 Priest, 1823 Papal diplomat in Chile, 1827 Bishop then Archbishop in the the Papal States, 1845 Cardinal.
1846 Surprise choice as Pope on the death of Gregory XVI. Took name of Pius IX (known in Italy as Pope Pio Nono). Was to be longest reign to date (1846–1878).
Appeared a liberal. Immediately freed 2000 political prisoners,

mostly revolutionaries; reformed education, the law and Papal administration; gave laymen greater share in public affairs.
1847 Ended censorship of press, allowed 100 mostly revolutionary newspapers, establishment of political clubs and formation in Rome of civic guard. Allowed Jews out of ghetto and granted Rome a constitution to replace absolute Papal rule. Created the *Consulta*, an elected body to advise the Pope.
1848 April 29 Complete change of policy. Suddenly condemned Italian nationalists, rejected the Risorgimento and refused to allow Papal troops to help drive out the Austrians. Had to escape in disguise from Rome as 1848–9 revolutions began.
1849 Excommunicated all who tried to reduce Temporal Power of Papacy and denounced Roman Republic.
1850 Returned to Rome. Abolished all early reforms.
1861 Catholics forbidden to have any connection with the new Kingdom of Italy.
Retired into the Vatican.
1864 Syllabus of Errors published. Rejected liberalism and other 'pernicious errors'.
1870 First Vatican Council held. Attempt to increase Pope's Spiritual Power, having lost most of the Temporal Power. Papal decisions declared infallible. Freedom of religion opposed. Catholic doctrine only true belief.
1878 Pius IX died within a month of Victor Emmanuel II, his long-standing enemy.
Task: compare the portrait of Pius IX (page 22) and the cartoon on page 23. What does it tell us about what the artist thought of the Pope? What event in the Pope's life do you think best fits the cartoon? Why? What political group would you expect the artist to support? Why? (You may need to look back at the list of political groups given at the beginning of this chapter).

short time before Piedmont began canvassing the other states with a proposal that Charles Albert should be the future king of a united Italy.

However, there was another possible leader suggested by the Piedmontese writer Gioberti who, in 1843, proposed that as the Pope and the Catholic Church were the glories of Italy, the Italian states should form themselves into a federation with the Pope as its President. Five thousand copies of his book were sold, but the bad reputation of the Papal States as oppressive and corrupt was too great a stumbling block for his ideas to be put into operation. However, the situation changed in 1846 with the election of a new Pope, Pius IX, who was believed to have liberal sympathies.

Pope Pius IX, 1875.

Pius IX was a man of personal piety and deep faith, but emotional, excitable and with a quick temper. He was seen by many who knew him as impressionable, impulsive and unpredictable. Pius said of himself in a letter to a previous Pope that due to his epilepsy he 'had a very weak memory and could not concentrate on a subject for any length of time without having to worry about his ideas getting terribly confused'. He was very easily influenced by stronger person- alities and was described by the British Ambassador in 1860 as having 'an amiable but weak mind'. He is remembered today for the length of his reign and for his firm stand on Catholic doctrine.

Pope Pius IX, cartoon of 1852.

7 The Revolutions of 1848–9

> **KEY ISSUE** Why did they fail?

The Pope's reforms in 1848 and early 1849 set an example to other states and their rulers. In Piedmont and Tuscany press censorship was abolished and proposals were made for a joint customs union with the Papal States. Even Austrian-controlled Lombardy became restless, worrying Metternich who acted swiftly to preserve Austrian control in northern Italy by making new treaties with Modena and Parma and by strengthening the Austrian garrison.

General discontent in Italy, the demands of the liberals for constitutions, for government reforms and political freedom in the individual states, and the continuous demands by nationalists for Italian unity and independence from Austria became ever louder.

About 90 per cent of the population of Italy worked on the land and the economy was based almost entirely on agriculture. There was little industry in the north and almost none in the south of the country. The harvests failed in 1846 and 1847 and were disastrous not only for the peasants but also for those in the towns. Shortages of wheat and maize meant high prices, wages did not rise to meet the increased costs, and peasants and others earning day wages could not afford to feed their families.

The result was an outbreak of revolutions, beginning in Sicily where Ferdinand II King of Naples had first offered a better life for Sicilians by making reforms and appointing a viceroy to see that the reforms were carried out. These did not last and a period of repression coinciding with an outbreak of cholera left the Sicilians in a desperate state.

In January 1848 notices were posted up in Palermo, the island's capital:

1 Sicilians! the time for prayers is past; peaceful protests and demonstrations have all been useless. Ferdinand, King of Naples, has treated them all with contempt and we, as people born free, are loaded with chains and reduced to misery. Shall we still delay claiming our lawful rights? To
5 arms, sons of Sicily; our united force will be invincible ... Heaven will not fail to support our just undertaking. Sicilians, to arms!

The notice went on to explain how people could obtain arms. They were to be handed out to those who came to the main piazza at dawn three days later (although in fact the organisers had not made proper arrangements for getting hold of arms, and only a few weapons were available). The authorities could not really believe that a revolution was being announced in advance, but they took no chances and arrested a few likely suspects.

On the day announced the streets were full of people, but

whether they were ordinary sightseers or revolutionaries it was impossible to say. After what arms were available had been handed out there were clashes with the government troops. Next day peasants from outside the city arrived to join in the rising. The Neapolitan army retaliated by shelling the city and were joined two days later by 5000 Neapolitan reinforcements. They found the revolutionaries had successfully taken over the city and were demanding a restoration of the famous 1812 constitution which had been abolished by the King of Naples in 1816. A compromise was offered. It was refused. Fighting continued and by April the revolutionaries had taken over most of the island. A provisional government was set up with the help of middle-class moderates who were becoming anxious about what the peasants might do next. A civic guard was formed to control 'the masses' who were marching on towns and villages, destroying property, freeing prisoners, and burning tax collection records. A Parliament was elected and declared that Naples and Sicily were finally totally separated and divided, and that the King of Naples was no longer King of Sicily. The Sicilians' aim was as always, in 1848 as in 1820, to free themselves from Naples. They were not concerned with national unity – quite the opposite. Theirs was a separatist movement with the aim of breaking away from Naples and making Sicily independent.

On the mainland, the revolution had spread to Naples within a few days of the uprising in Palermo. A huge demonstration demanded a constitution. The King agreed to a two-chamber parliament with limited power. He also agreed to form a national guard and to free the press from censorship, but peasant grievances over their right to use common land led to fighting which was quickly suppressed. By September the government in Naples was able to send troops to retake Sicily. The Sicilians were defeated and by the spring of 1849 were forced to accept reunification with Naples. There the King had already gone back on his earlier promises, abolished parliament and replaced it with absolute rule and a police state.

In other parts of Italy other serious disturbances were occuring in 1848. As a result the Grand Duke of Tuscany and the King of Piedmont promised to grant constitutions. Their example was soon followed by the Pope, but in Modena and Parma the rulers had to leave their states. Trouble also started in Milan in Austrian-controlled Lombardy. It began as a tobacco boycott. Tobacco was an Austrian state monopoly and the people of Milan believed that if they stopped smoking Austrian finances would be seriously affected. The sight of Austrian soldiers smoking in public was an excuse for attacking them and small-scale fights quickly turned into larger riots and eventually into a full-scale revolution known as 'The Five Days' (17–22 March). The Austrian commander, 81-year-old General Radetsky (remembered now for the march tune bearing his name) decided to withdraw from the city, not because he was defeated, but because the situation in Austria had changed dramatically. Revolution had broken out in Vienna and Metternich had been dismissed. The provisional government set up in Milan by the revolutionaries prepared to continue the fight against Austria. They decided to ask for help from Charles Albert, King of Piedmont, who had just granted a constitution to his people. A week later, Charles Albert agreed to declare war on Austria and the provisional government in Milan issued an emotional and inaccurate appeal to their fellow citizens:

1 We have conquered. We have compelled the enemy to fly, oppressed as much by his own shame as our valour; but scattered in our fields, wandering like wild beasts, united in bands of plunderers, he prolonged for us the horrors of war without affording any of its sublime emotions.
5 This makes it easy to understand that the arms we have taken up, and still hold, can never be laid down as long as one of his band shall be hid under cover of the Alps. We have sworn, we swear it again, with the generous Prince who flies to associate himself with our glory – all Italy swears it and so it shall be.
10 To arms then, to arms, to secure the fruits of our glorious revolution – to fight the last battle of independence and the Italian Union.

In the other Austrian-controlled state, Venetia, a small-scale revolt persuaded the Austrians to surrender, and the Independent Venetian Republic of St. Mark was proclaimed in March. Its rapidly elected assembly voted for union with Piedmont.

At first all went well with Charles Albert. His army defeated the Austrians at the end of May 1848 but in the Papal States, things were not going so well. The Pope's army commander had disobeyed orders and set off with his troops to join Charles Albert's army. This made difficulties for the Pope who was not at war with Austria. He decided to keep out of the war against Austria and, to make his position clear, issued an Allocution, an official policy speech made to senior Churchmen:

1 ... But seeing that some at present desire that We too, along with the other Princes of Italy and their subjects, should engage in war against the Austrians, We have thought it suitable to proclaim clearly and openly in this our solemn Assembly, that such a measure is altogether
5 alien from our counsels, in as much as We albeit unworthy, are upon earth the viceregent of Him that is the Author of Peace and Lover of Charity....
We cannot refrain from dissociating ourselves from the treacherous advice published in journals, and various works, of those who want the
10 Roman Pontiff (the Pope) to be the head of and to preside over some sort of novel Republic of the whole Italian people. On this occasion we do urgently warn the Italian people to have no part in these proposals, which would be ruinous to Italy, but live in loyalty to their sovereigns whose goodwill they have already experienced, and never to let them-
15 selves be torn away. If they do otherwise, they would not only fail in

their duty, but would also run the risk of rending Italy herself, everyday more and more, with fresh disagreements and revolutionary activities.

The Allocution not only made it clear that the Pope would not join in the war against Austria, but also that he was no longer interested in the idea of becoming head of an Italian federation of states, or even in the idea of the Church lending support for a united Italy. Two years earlier the Pope had 'blessed "Italy"'. He now withdrew his blessing. The Church had turned her back on liberalism and gone over to the side of reaction and absolutism. For Charles Albert and other loyal Catholics the loss of Papal support for their cause was a bitter blow. They would have to choose between following their political principles and obeying their spiritual leader. It was a difficult decision but many decided in favour of their political principles. As a result the liberal and nationalist movements became noticeably anti-clerical, that is, unsympathetic in their attitude to the Church and its teachings.

By June of 1848 reinforcements had arrived from Austria and in July Charles Albert's army was defeated by the Austrians at Custoza. An armistice was signed and Piedmont withdrew from Lombardy, leaving it in Austrian hands. The Venetians hurriedly cancelled their recently completed union with Piedmont, re-established the former Republic of St. Mark and prepared to continue the war with Austria. At this moment Mazzini arrived back in Italy. The 'war of the Princes' against Austria had failed; now it was time for the 'War of the People'.

8 The Roman Republic and the Revolutions of 1848–9

> **KEY ISSUES** Why did revolutions continue to fail in 1848–9? What could have been done to make them a success?

In Rome the Pope's unpopular chief minister was murdered at the end of November. Rioting followed and the Pope fled from a city in turmoil to take refuge in Naples, while the government which he had left behind announced a series of reforms. They abolished the unpopular tax on grinding corn, provided public building work for the unemployed and proposed the holding of a *Constituente*, a meeting in Rome of representatives from all over Italy. The election of these representatives was organised by a special Council of State whose members were chosen by the government of Rome, and the *Constituente* met for the first time in February 1849. Among its members was Garibaldi. Four days later the *Constituente* proclaimed an end to the Temporal Power of the Pope and the establishment of the Roman Republic.

In March Mazzini arrived in Rome and was elected as head of the

Revolutions 1820–49

Triumvirate, a group of three men who would rule the city. This they did in a fair, tolerant and enlightened way for the remaining months of the Republic's life. The Pope appealed to France, Spain and Naples to help free Rome 'from the enemies of our most holy religion and civil society', and an army of about 20,000 men was sent from the French Republic to destroy the Roman Republic. This they did, for although the gallant defence of the city by Garibaldi became one of the legends of the Risorgimento, the odds against him were too great and the city fell to the French at the end of June 1849. A French garrison with the duty of safeguarding the Pope remained in Rome until 1870.

Mazzini explained why the Roman Republic fought so fiercely:

1 To the many other causes which decided us to resist, there was one closely bound up with the aim of my whole life – the foundation of a national unity. Rome was the natural centre of that unity and it was important to attract the eyes and reverence of my countrymen towards
5 her... It was essential to redeem Rome; to place her once again at the summit so that Italians might again learn to regard her as the temple of their common country ... I had faith in her ... the defence of the city was therefore decided upon; by the assembly and people of Rome from a noble impulse and from reverence for the honour of Italy; by me as
10 the logical consequence of a long-matured design.

After the fall of the city he appealed to citizens:

1 Romans your city has been overcome by brute force, but your rights are neither lessened nor changed. By all you hold sacred, citizens, keep yourselves uncontaminated. Organise peaceful demonstrations. Let your local district councils unceasingly declare with calm firmness that
5 they voluntarily adhere to the Republican form of government and the abolition of the Temporal Power of the Pope; and that they regard as illegal whatever government may be imposed without the free approval of the people ... In the streets, in the theatres, in every place of meeting let the same cries be heard. Thousands cannot be imprisoned. Men
10 cannot be compelled to degrade themselves.

The Pope returned to Rome in the afternoon of 12 April 1850 and was cheered through the streets by the same citizens who had cheered for Mazzini, Garibaldi and the Roman Republic a year earlier, clear evidence that for most people the ending of the hardships they had endured in the past months under French military occupation was preferable to vague hopes of national independence and unity proclaimed by Mazzini and his associates.

The Roman Republic was not alone. There was another, the Venetian Republic, that had held out courageously against a siege by the Austrian navy in the cource of which the city was heavily shelled in the early summer of 1849. A severe outbreak of cholera added to the misery of starving Venetians who were driven by their hunger and disease to surrender to the Austrians in August 1849.

Earlier in the year Charles Albert, having apparently recovered from the horrors of his defeat at Custoza and his distress at abandoning Lombardy to the Austrians, decided in March to re-enter the war. Exactly why he made this decision is not clear. Some historians believe he wanted revenge for his earlier defeat, others think that it was because he had had time to regroup his forces and was ready for action. He may also have believed, wrongly, that France would come to his aid if he re-entered the war.

He was not to get his revenge. Within a month he was heavily defeated at the battle of Novara. This was the last straw. A broken man, he abdicated in favour of his son, Victor Emmanuel II.

In neighbouring Tuscany the Grand Duke had granted a constitution at the beginning of 1848. When news of the revolution in Vienna and the dismissal of Metternich reached Tuscany, the government decided to send a small army to fight the Austrians. Workers in the cities began to agitate about pay and conditions and middle-class radical extremists began to preach republicanism. In January 1849 the Grand Duke could stand it no longer and left for Naples with its still absolute monarchy. In Tuscany a revolutionary provisional government was set up and a dictator was appointed in advance of arrangements being made to proclaim a republic. Before this could be done, however, Charles Albert had been defeated at Novara. This left the Austrian army free to sweep down into Tuscany where they crushed the revolution and restored the Grand Duke to his throne. Much the same happened in Modena and Parma, where their rulers who fled to escape the revolutions were also restored to their thrones by Austrian military might.

KEY ISSUE Why the 1848–9 revolutions failed.

By the middle of 1849 it was clear that the revolutions had failed, just as they had in 1820 and 1831. In Sicily Neapolitan rule had been re-established and the Two Sicilies forcibly reunited under an even more absolute and repressive government than before. In the Papal States the Roman Republic had been destroyed, the Pope restored to his temporal power by the French soldiers who continued to occupy Rome. All expectations that Pius IX would be a liberal supporter of national unity for Italy were totally shattered. Tuscany, Modena and Parma found themselves again under absolute rule. The Venetian Republic came under tighter Austrian control as did Lombardy, and, worst of all, the strongest state, Piedmont, had suffered humiliating defeat by the Austrians in two battles. The only success for the revolutionaries was that the constitution, the *Statuto,* granted to Piedmont by Charles Albert, survived and would continue to do so, eventually becoming the basis of the consitution of the new united Kingdom of Italy in 1860. None of the other constitutions wrung from their rulers by the revolutionaries did so. None of the rulers forced to escape from their states were away for long. None of the states which gained independence – Sicily, Lombardy and Venetia – was able to retain it.

The revolutions had been an almost total failure, and a failure which had involved suffering and death for a very large number of people. As in the earlier revolutions there was a lack of cooperation between the revolutionary groups. Those in Sicily and Naples were at loggerheads. In Piedmont Charles Albert would not accept volunteers from other states in his army nor work with any other revolutionary groups unless they first declared their loyalty to the Piedmontese royal family.

The revolutionaries themselves were divided on domestic policies. Liberals believed that the granting of a constitution by the ruler was the necessary first step everywhere. Constitutional government was essential to the development of Italian nationalism. The radicals disagreed. Their policy was the eventual formation of an Italian republic, but as most active revolutionaries were moderate liberals, constitutional government continued to be the first priority in the majority of revolutions. Liberals and radicals though were united in their other aims – expelling the foreign occupying power, Austria, and the creation of a united and independent Italy. The only questions were how and by whom?

There was unfortunately no universally acceptable national leader who could coordinate policy. Of the three possible candidates, Mazzini, Pope Pius IX and Charles Albert, none was appointed. If one of them had been, it might have been even worse than having none, because they each had different political ideas. Local revolutionary leaders had no central guidance and the provisional (temporary) governments which they set up could be moderate, extremist, liberal, radical, republican, democratic or monarchist.

In the end it was not just that the provisional governments lacked guidance. They were inexperienced, weak and lacking in resources, particularly military ones. They could not maintain themselves in power having gained it, partly due to lack of support from the mass of the population, except perhaps while fighting was actually going on. The liberals did not in any case wish to encourage popular support or to involve the pesants. Politics, for liberals, was a middle-class affair. With few exceptions peasants found themselves no better off under a liberal-dominated revolutionary government than they had been before. Social reform was not important to liberals and life did not improve for ordinary people. As a result they welcomed back, more enthusiastically than expected, rulers who had been dispossessed. The republics successfully established by radicals in Venetia and Rome were destroyed by the military power of Austria and France.

The military supremacy of Austria was probably the single most important factor in the failure of the revolutions. The Austrian armies were superior in numbers, better equipped and much better led than any other army in the peninsula. In any conflict they were bound to win, even if the revolutionary forces had been able to present a united front – which they did not. It was by Austrian and, to a lesser extent, French military involvement that the old regimes were restored in 1849.

The Italian situation was unexpectedly about to change for the better in the 1850s. In Piedmont the *Statuto* remained in force and gave opportunities for political life to continue in ways which were not possible elsewhere in Italy. Refugees from other states came to Piedmont and settled there, more than 200,000 in Turin and Genoa. They gave Piedmont a cosmopolitan air and a more nationalist flavour which paved the way for what was to come in the person of Count Camillo Benso di Cavour. He was to be one of the great figures in the history of the unification of Italy before his untimely death in 1861.

Reference

Lucy Riall, *The Italian Risorgimento* (Routledge, 1994), Chapter 2.

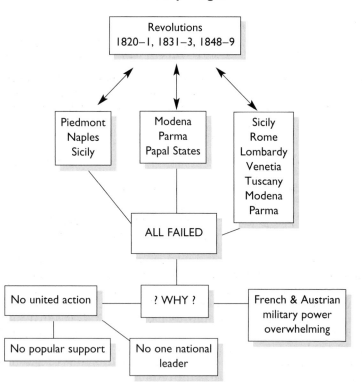

Summary Diagram

Working on Chapter 2

Chapter 2 includes coverage of several topics frequently chosen as the basis of examination questions. These include the contribution of Giuseppe Mazzini to the cause of Italian unification, the background and causes of the revolutions in Italy in 1848–9, the reasons for the failure of those revolutions and the significance of the role of Pope Pius IX. The chapter also provides details of the barriers to Italian unification. As these do not appear as a single topic it would be useful if you made your own notes under the following headings: traditions of localism and separatism; the self-interest of the numerous states; natural barriers and the geography of the country; lack of uniformity in administration (different currencies, customs houses etc.); autocratic rule (particularly in the Two Sicilies and Papal States); differing schools of thought regarding how unification might be achieved. You will also need to consider the extent to which Austria and France were involved in the affairs of the Italian states. Finally note the stages by which Piedmont emerged as the state best suited to lead the struggle to achieve unification, and consider, after the failures of 1848–9, the direction this struggle might follow.

Answering structured questions on Chapter 2

There is little in the chapter that would allow questions to be set that might cover the whole period 1820–49. Consequently, structured, document-based and essay questions are likely to be taken from relatively narrow topic areas.
A typical structured question might be:

I. **a)** Explain briefly the differences in the aims and views of Italian liberals and nationalists? (*4 marks*)
   b) To what extent were Metternich's policies aimed at keeping the Italian states weak and divided? (*6 marks*)
   c) For what reasons did Pope Pius IX change his attitude to the issue of Italian unification? Explain your answer fully. (*10 marks*)

Question a) is easily answered by reference to pages 10–11. At the same time examine once again the different views held by Italian radicals and republicans. In answering b), carefully note Metternich's attitude to liberalism and nationalism. Why did he hold such views? Explaining the change of attitude of Pope Pius IX is difficult. Read pages 20–23 again and make notes about the reasons for the high hopes held by Italian nationalists following the Pope's unexpected election in 1846 and the extent of his change of attitude barely two years later.

Answering source-based questions on Chapter 2

Read carefully the notice that appeared in the streets of Palermo in 1848 (page 24) and the appeal made by the Piedmontese provisional government in Milan during the same year (page 26). Remember that in question c), which requires you to evaluate the extracts, it is necessary to bear in mind the possible bias of their authors. Answer the following questions:

a) (i) In the first extract, explain what is meant by 'we, as people born free, are loaded with chains and reduced to misery' (*2 marks*)
   (ii) In the second extract, explain what is meant by 'as long as one of his band shall be hid under the cover of the Alps' (*2 marks*)
b) To what extent do the two extracts agree that it is necessary for Italians to resort to arms in order to achieve their aims (*6 marks*)
c) How useful are the two extracts to an understanding of the events that led to the revolutions in Italy in 1848–49? Explain your answer fully. (*10 marks*)

Answering essay questions on Chapter 2

1. 'His contribution to the cause of Italian unification was negligible'. How valid is this assessment of Mazzini? (*25 marks*)
2. To what extent might it be claimed that lack of cooperation between the Italian states was the main barrier to Italian unification? (*25 marks*)
3. 'The uprisings in Italy during 1848–9 failed because they lacked the support of the Papacy'. How valid is this statement? (*25 marks*)

In question 1 it is necessary to make an estimate of Mazzini's contribution to Italian unification. Was he merely a great thinker? What did he actually achieve? Later, when you have progressed further into the book, you will be able to measure his achievements against those of the other great champions of the *Risorgimento*, Cavour and Garibaldi. Before attempting question 2, read again the notes you have made on the barriers to Italian unity. The question does not simply require you to examine and explain them. You need to gauge lack of cooperation against the other obstacles to unification and decide if it was the 'main' barrier. Similarly in question 3, it is necessary to go beyond examining the reasons for the failure of the revolutions in 1848–9! Was lack of backing by Pope Pius IX the main contributory factor? More interestingly, do you think the revolutions would have succeeded had they had his support? Were there other factors that outweighed this?

Working on multi-source questions on Chapter 2

Questions based on multi-sources are often considered the most difficult set in an examination paper. This is because you not only have to show an understanding of the sources used but, in addition, have to be able to compare sources, assess their reliability and evaluate them. It is also necessary to take the authorship or provenance of the sources into consideration. The sources used may be either primary or secondary and might include the use of documents (extracts from speeches, letters and written works) as well as illustrations, cartoons, maps and statistics.

Source Exercise – Events in Italy during 1848

Source A

1 'When I left Venice in November, everything was perfectly quiet ... Now, however, it is quite different; the Venetians have adopted the system of the Milanese, and there is hardly a Venetian house into which an Austrian is admitted. Persons supposed to have a leaning towards
5 the government have their names written upon walls as traitors to their country. Should a collision ensue between the troops and the people ... the outcome, I fear, could be very serious.'

[From a dispatch sent by the British Consul-General in Venice to London in January 1848.]

Source B

1 'Events have been brought about by the brutality of the police and the ferocity of Radetzky. Four months ago I could never have believed that hatred could have spread everywhere so fast... The armies of spies have been doubled. People live in continual fear of being arrested even
5 on the slightest excuse... We rely on Piedmont to save us.'

[From a letter written by a Milanese statesman in February 1848.]

Source C

1 'My information from the provinces, though slight, is very alarming, for the whole country is in revolt and even the peasants are armed. The armistice is not concluded and fighting continues with unabated fury ... all communications are interrupted ... and my units meet strong
5 resistance in the barricaded streets and villages.'

[From a dispatch sent by Field Marshal Radetzky to Vienna in March 1848.]

Source D

1 The supreme hour of the Piedmontese monarchy has struck, the hour of stern decisions, the hour on which hangs the fate of empires, the destiny of nations. Faced with the events in Lombardy and Vienna, hesitation, doubt and delay are no longer possible, they would prove the

5 most fatal of policies ... One road alone is now open to the nation ...
War! Immediate war! War without delay!

[From an article written by Count Cavour in March 1848.]

Source E

1 It is not with shouts or with applause that we should fight the enemies
of our country, but with weapons and the shedding of blood. Every con-
ceivable weapon, whether a gun, a dagger, a scythe, a stick, everything
should be used in our war against these contemptible assassins from
5 Austria.'

[From a speech made by Giuseppe Garibaldi in 1848.]

a) **(i)** What do Sources A and B reveal about the relationship between
the Austrians and Italians living under their rule? (5 marks)
(ii) Comment on the reliability of Sources A and C. (5 marks)
b) **(i)** Compare Sources D and E. To what extent do they agree on the
measures needed to expel the Austrians from Italy? (5 marks)
(ii) Compare Sources A, B and C. To what extent do Sources B and
C share the fears expressed by the British Consul General in
Source A? (5 marks)
c) How full understanding do the sources provide of events in Italy during
1848? In your answer use your own relevant knowledge as well as
information derived from the sources. (10 marks)

3 Piedmont, Cavour and Italy

POINTS TO CONSIDER

As you read through this quite complicated chapter there are four things to consider. How did the 'poor and backward state of Piedmont' come to be, by 1860, the strongest and most important of the Italian states, able to put itself and its king at the head of the newly united and independent Italy? What sort of person was Cavour? Could unification have been achieved without him? How successfully did he deal with what he saw as a threat from Garibaldi in the south?

KEY DATES

1720	Dukes of Savoy, rulers of Piedmont, become also Kings of Sardinia.
1802–1814	Piedmont united with France.
1811	Cavour born.
1815	Victor Emmanuel I returned to Piedmont as one of the Restored Monarchs.
1815	Genoa united with Piedmont.
1820	Revolution in Piedmont unsuccessful – Victor Emmanuel I abdicated.
	Charles Felix became king.
1831	Charles Felix died. Succeeded by Charles Albert.
1848	*The Statuto* proclaimed. Charles Albert declared war on Austria.
	Defeated at Custoza and in 1849 at Novara.
1849	Charles Albert abdicated. Succeeded by Victor Emmanuel II.
1852	Cavour became Prime Minister.
1858	Plombières meeting and agreement with Napoleon III to force war on Austria.
1859	France and Piedmont at war with Austria. Battles of Magenta and Solferino.
	War ended with armistice of Villafranca arranged by Napoleon III. Cavour resigned.
1860	Cavour returned. Again Prime Minister.
	Garibaldi's conquest of southern Italy.
1861	Victor Emmanuel proclaimed King of Italy. Death of Cavour.

1 Piedmont

> **KEY ISSUE** From an unpromising start, how did Piedmont become the most powerful state in Italy by 1860? Was this due to her kings, her politicians, her soldiers, or to France?

In 1720 the Dukes of Savoy who ruled over the then poor and backward state of Piedmont in northwest Italy became kings of the island of Sardinia. Piedmont and Sardinia together came to be known as the Kingdom of Sardinia, or Sardinia Piedmont, but most usually just as Piedmont.

At the end of the eighteenth century Piedmont had only a small population, most of whom were peasants. Although a large number of children were born, the death rate was very high and life was short. The number of people living in the capital, Turin, was declining, there was little or no industry, and the countryside was poverty-stricken. However, Piedmont had two advantages over neighbouring states. It had a very strong army unlike the other states, and was well governed by an absolute monarch. The king as head of state made all the decisions, all the laws, decided the taxes and what they should be spent on and appointed the government. He alone could declare war or make peace. There was no parliament so the people had no share in government, no votes and no say in what happened.

At the end of the eighteenth century Piedmont made an alliance with Austria. The Piedmontese royal family was closely connected by marriage with the French royal family and this made them automatically an enemy of Napoleon and the French Republic. In 1792, when the French army attacked Nice and Savoy to the west of Piedmont, Austria and Piedmont declared war on France. The war went badly for the allies with the result that during 1799 and again from 1802 to 1814 Piedmont was united with France. This meant that Piedmont came into very close contact with French law and French government organisation. Piedmontese schools became part of the French education system and Piedmont's young men were conscripted (forced to serve) in the French army. French became the language of polite society as well as of government, and the well-to-do members of society became more and more French in outlook. There was no great opposition to French rule and the middle classes even found it to their advantage in providing career opportunities. In government service and in the army, they were allowed to fill posts previously reserved only for members of the nobility.

Only towards the end of French occupation was there unrest and dissatisfaction and young men setting up anti-French secret societies.

In 1815 the king of Piedmont, Victor Emmanuel I, who had been in exile during the Napoleonic years, returned to Turin as one of the Restored Monarchs (see page 6). To make himself more welcome he abolished conscription and reduced taxation, but following his ministers' advice he announced that Piedmont was still bound by the out-of-date laws made before 1800, and that these could not now be changed. Piedmont became once again an absolute monarchy. The French legal system, the Code Napoleon, was abolished along with equal justice for all. Criminal trials were no longer open or fair, the only good thing being that torture was not reintroduced. The Vienna

Settlement of 1815 had given Piedmont control of the former Republic of Genoa and this was of great commercial benefit to Piedmont, for Genoa was an important port. The Genoese, however, were not impressed. They resented the loss of their former independence, particularly when Piedmont introduced new regulations which hampered Genoese trade.

a) Charles Albert

In 1819 just as local and central government were being modernised in Piedmont, the alarms about the possibility of a revolution led to modernisation being brought to a sudden end. Membership of revolutionary secret societies was growing at this time and some moderate Piedmontese hoped that this would encourage the king to introduce political and other reforms. They were disappointed but not surprised, knowing there was little chance of action by Victor Emmanuel I or his brother and heir Charles Felix. They turned therefore to the second in line to the throne, Charles Albert.

Charles Albert was a strange, rather quiet young man, who had been brought up in exile in France. On his return to Piedmont he saw just how severe and oppressive Victor Emmanuel's government had become. Charles Albert showed sympathy with revolutionary students injured in riots in Turin and was known to have connections with revolutionary officers in the army. In March 1821 the liberals (moderate non-violent reformers) appealed to him to lead a revolution, and it seems that he agreed to do so, although he later denied it. Perhaps he really did intend to lead the revolution and only denied it when it failed. There are also suggestions, though there is no clear evidence for it, that he may have been acting as a government agent and only pretending to be in sympathy with the revolutionaries in order to gather information about their plans. Such action would be in keeping with his secretive personality. Perhaps, and probably most likely, he had not made up his mind and just dithered as he hesitated between two or more possible courses of action. 'The legend of Charles Albert' as someone who could not make up his mind had begun.

While he was dithering a revolutionary group seized the fortress of Alessandria in Genoa and established a provisional (temporary) government calling itself the 'Kingdom of Italy' and, rather foolishly, declaring war on Austria. This declaration came to nothing because Victor Emmanuel, tired of being pressured by revolutionary groups to grant political and social reforms, and worried by reports of new army mutinies in Turin, decided to abdicate. He left for Nice, close to the western frontier of Piedmont, as revolution spread throughout his kingdom. His brother and heir, Charles Felix, succeeded him, but died in 1831. This left his son Charles Albert to become, at last, King of Piedmont.

It looked as though his reign was to be as absolute and oppressive as that of Victor Emmanuel's, for despite his flirtation with the rebels, in 1821 Charles Albert began his reign as a reactionary monarch, by signing a treaty with Austria and threatening to attack the Liberal goverment then in power in France. All was to change, for by 1848–9 Charles Albert was to grant his people a constitution which would survive to be the constitution of the united Italy of the 1860s.

Historians have tried to explain why Charles Albert changed from a reactionary to a liberal, but have not found any satisfactory answer. One suggestion is that he had always been a nationalist, perhaps even a secret revolutionary, and once king, was waiting only for a suitable opportunity to declare himself. This is not very convincing. More probably the answer lies in Charles Albert's own complicated character.

His whole career was one of contradictions. He seems to have been secretive and unsociable, seldom showing any emotion. A devout Christian, he wore a hair shirt and was much attracted to the more mystical aspects of the Catholic Church. He believed, mistakenly, that he was cut out to be a soldier and a leader of men. He could be energetic and enterprising on a short-term basis, but lacked long-term determination. Most important of all, his view of life was entirely divorced from reality.

His policies in the early years of his reign show how uncertain were his political beliefs. On the one hand he refused to pardon the political prisoners left over from the 1821 revolutions, and increased the power of the Church in Piedmont. He increased also the already severe censorship laws so that Mazzini and Garibaldi left Piedmont, soon to be followed by Gioberti who, anxious to publish his proposals for a federation of Italian states presided over by the Pope, soon left for the liberal city of Brussels. Cavour too left Piedmont, 'that intellectual hell', preferring the greater freedom of expression found almost anywhere else, including Austrian Lombardy.

On the other hand, some of Charles Albert's early actions were those of a reformer. He made helpful changes in trade laws, reduced duties on imported goods and signed trade treaties with other states. He tidied up the legal system and its laws, and allowed non-nobles to fill senior posts in the army and the royal advisory council.

During the 1840s influences from other parts of Italy crept slowly into Piedmont. In 1841 social, non-political groups were allowed to meet freely for the first time. These groups were unimportant in themselves. Their importance lay in the fact that they existed at all and represented a small step forward to a more relaxed regime. Piedmont also hosted at this time a number of scientific congresses, which helped to spread nationalist ideas, especially as at one congress held in 1846 Charles Albert was referred to as 'the Italian leader who would drive out the foreigners'.

Unfortunately Charles Albert took to heart this idea of himself as a military leader and from now on seems to have thought, with what were to be disastrous results, that his future was that of the military genius who would destroy the Austrian hold on Lombardy and Venetia.

As the 1840s went by, the pressure for liberal reforms grew. In Turin there were peaceful demands for a constitution from the small but well-educated and outspoken middle and professional social classes. In Genoa where the republican Mazzini was well known and greatly respected for his views, demands were more violent and revolutionary. The unrest in Turin spread, ending in October 1847 in noisy demonstrations and threats of revolution which persuaded Charles Albert to agree to make reforms and to grant a constitution early in 1848. As a devout Catholic he was probably influenced by the limited reforms recently introduced by the Pope into the Papal States.

Charles Albert's general reforms were aimed at taking some of the power away from the monarchy and putting it into the hands of government officials. For instance, the police were in future to be under the control of the Minister of the Interior. Local government was also reorganised and local councils elected.

The constitution which Charles Albert had promised was issued in the form of 14 articles on 8 February 1848, and was known as the *Statuto:*

1 Now, therefore, that the times are ripe for greater things and, in the midst of the changes which have occurred in Italy, we hestitate no longer to give our people the most solemn proof that we are able to give of the faith which we continue to repose in their devotion and dis-
5 cretion ...
... for the present we have much pleasure in declaring that, with the advice and approval of our Ministers and the principal advisers of our Crown, we have resolved and determined to adopt the following bases of a fundamental statute for the establishment in our states of a com-
10 plete system of representative Government.
Article 1. The Catholic, Apostolic and Roman religion is the sole religion of the state.
The other forms of public worship at present existing are tolerated in conformity with the laws.
15 *Article 2* The person of the Sovereign is sacred and inviolable. His ministers are responsible.
Article 3 To the King alone belongs the executive power. He is the supreme head of the State. He commands all the forces both naval and military; declares war, concludes treaties of peace, alliance and com-
20 merce; nominates to all offices, and gives all the necessary orders for the execution of the laws without suspending or dispensing with the observance thereof.
Article 4 The King alone sanctions and promulgates laws.
Article 5 All justice emanates from the King and is administered in his
25 name. He may grant mercy and commute punishment.

Article 6 The legislative power will be collectively exercised by the King and the two Chambers.

Article 7 The first of these Chambers will be composed of members nominated by the King for life; the second will be elective, on the basis
30 of the census to be determined.

Article 8 The proposal of laws will appertain to the King and to each of the Chambers but with the distinct understanding that all laws imposing taxes must originate in the elective Chamber.

Article 9 The King convokes the two Chambers annually, prorogues
35 their sessions and may dissolve the elective one; but in this case he will convoke a new assembly at the expiration of four months.

Article 10 No tax may be imposed or levied if not assented to by the Chambers and sanctioned by the King.

Article 11 The press will be free but subject to restraining laws.
40 *Article 12* Individual liberty will be guaranteed.

Article 13 The judges ... will be irremovable, after having exercised their functions for a certain space of time, to be hereafter determined.

Article 14 We reserve to ourselves the power of establishing a district militia ... composed of persons who may pay a rate, which will be fixed
45 hereafter. This militia will be placed under the command of the administrative authority, and in dependence on the Minister of the Interior. The King will have the power of suspending or dissolving it in places where he may deem it opportune so to do....

These articles were not very clearly expressed and some historians believe that this was intentional. It was a way for Charles Albert to avoid giving too much of his power away, while also keeping his options open. Phrases like 'The King's Ministers are responsible' left it uncertain to whom or for what they were responsible – to the King? to the Chambers? Equally unclear is the reference to the 'restraining laws' limiting the freedom of the press. We do not know exactly what these laws were, but they probably were some form of censorship.

The full *Statuto* was published in March 1848 and included a number of other clauses relating to legal equality for all, whatever their religion, and for equal employment opportunities. It did not decide who was going to have the vote to elect members of the Lower Chamber. This was fixed later when the vote was given to men who could read and write and who paid taxes – about two per cent of the population of Piedmont.

The constitution was not a Parliamentary one except in a very limited way, because it allowed the King to keep most of his existing rights. Nevertheless, many of Charles Albert's ministers thought it too extreme and were replaced by more liberal-minded men.

Why did Charles Albert decide to grant the *Statuto*? Was he sincere in wanting to give his people more say in government, or did he simply want to make a popular revolution less likely? Had it been his aim all along to grant a constitution, or did he have a sudden change of heart? Historians argue about his motives, but so far fail to agree.

Meanwhile, events outside Piedmont were moving rapidly and may have influenced Charles Albert's decision to proclaim the constitution. Revolutions in Sicily, Naples, Lombardy and Venetia broke out in rapid succession. In Austrian Lombardy extreme revolutionaries wanted an independent republic, while more moderate ones wanted union with Piedmont. Charles Albert saw advantages in putting himself at the head of a Lombard revolt against Austria, because this could lead to an eventual take over of Lombardy by Piedmont. Typically though he hesitated, undecided whether to take military action or not, afraid that his absence might allow his own revolutionaries to stir up trouble in Genoa, the part of Piedmont most likely to organise a revolution. Eventually public pressure and news that the revolutionary government now established in Venetia had voted for union with Piedmont persuaded *Il Re Tentenua* (the wobbling king) to declare war on 23 March '... for the purpose of more fully showing by outward signs the sentiments of Italian unity, we wish that our troops should enter the territory of Lombardy and Venetia, bearing the arms of Savoy (the royal family of Piedmont) above the Italian tri-coloured flag'.

Again historians have argued about Charles Albert's motives in going to war. Did he act out of self-interest in the expectation of Lombardy and Venetia being 'fused' with Piedmont as the price of his help? Or was he genuinely concerned to support a revolt against the foreigner, Austria, and make himself leader of a national independence movement? A year earlier he had written, 'Should providence call us to a war for the independence of Italy I will mount my horse and with my sons put myself at the head of my army ... glorious will be the day on which we can raise the cry of a war of Italian independence'. But that was at a time when such a war seemed unlikely.

The decision to act finally made, Charles Albert entered the war with enthusiasm. His army of 60,000 men, incompetently led by himself and ill prepared for war, crossed into Lombardy and occupied the capital, Milan. The Austrians, who had already evacuated the city, brought up reinforcements and defeated Charles Albert at Custoza on the border with Venetia. The King had no choice but to ask for an armistice. This allowed the Piedmontese army to withdraw from Lombardy, leaving it again in Austrian hands.

Charles Albert broke the news to his people in a carefully edited version of events:

1 My army was almost alone in the struggle. The want of provisions forced us to abandon the positions we had conquered ... for even the strength of the brave soldier has its limits. But the throbs of my heart were ever for Italian independence. People of the kingdom show your-
5 selves strong in a first misfortune ... have confidence in your king. The cause of Italian independence is not yet lost.

Early in 1849 having regrouped his forces, and been persuaded, incorrectly, by his chief minister that Louis Napoleon, newly elected President of the French Republic would come to his aid if Piedmont again attacked Austria, Charles Albert re-entered the war with as little success as before. He was heavily defeated by the Austrians at Novara in April.

His long cherished belief that Italy would gain her independence and unity by her own efforts alone '*Italia fara da se*' (Italy will make herself by herself) became nothing more than an empty boast. While Austria remained so powerful there was no way in which Italy could gain independence or unity without outside help.

One of the few survivors of 1848-9 was the Piedmontese *Statuto* embodying the constitution. Charles Albert was suceeded by his son Victor Emmanuel II who has traditionally been seen as a courageus figure defying Austrian plans for the *Statuto*'s abolition. Most historians now think that Victor Emmanuel was not particularly anxious to keep the constitution but was pressured into doing so by the Austrians themselves, who feared that if he got rid of it he would become so unpopular that not only he but the monarchy itself would be threatened. In Austrian eyes anything, even a state with a moderately liberal constitution, was better than a republic. The constitution, such as it was, therefore remained in force, and in spite of its limitations gave an opportunity for an active political life in Piedmont, something which did not then exist anywhere else in Italy. With a reasonably free press, an elected if unrepresentative assembly, and a certain amount of civil liberty and legal equality, Piedmont attracted refugees from the rest of Italy during the next decade, which was to be dominated by the political leadership of the now returned Cavour, the military successes of Garibaldi and the interventions of Napoleon III of France.

2 Cavour

> **KEY ISSUES** How is Cavour best described a) as a man and b) as a politician? How important was he in the creation of a united and independent Italy ?

Count Camillo Benso di Cavour was born in Piedmont in 1811 while it was still ruled by Napoleon. He was the second son of a rich Piedmontese noble, and his father, an intelligent and successful business man, was a minster in the government of Victor Emmanuel I. Cavour was sent away to the Royal Military Academy when he was ten. He proved to be a rebellious student and always in trouble. After leaving there he was for a short time in the service of Charles Albert, and then became an officer in the army, where again he had a reputation as a rebel. To get rid of him he was sent to a frontier post, where boredom led him to develop an interest in reading, mainly books on economics and politics. He even imagined himself to be Prime Minister of a united Italy, a totally unrealistic ambition in 1832, and not taken seriously by anyone. At the time he had no intention of going into politics.

He and the army parted company with no regrets on either side in 1833, and the next year, having no settled job, he set out to visit Paris and London. In Britain, Cavour visited the industrial cities of the north and was much impressed by the factories and mills he saw there. Not at all put off by the squalor, smoke and dirt, he particularly enjoyed the Liverpool–Manchester railway, the first passenger line in the world, which had been opened only five years earlier. For the rest of his life railways and railway travel remained an important interest.

In 1835 he returned to Piedmont and for a while engaged himself in his other great life-long interest, gambling on the stock exchange, in casinos and at cards. He then took over running part of the family estate, taking a practical interest in it, importing artificial fertilisers from America and making use of new agricultural methods and machinery. For 13 years while living on the estate he continued his study of economics and politics and began writing articles on a wide range of subjects. In 1846 he wrote on his favourite subject, railways, which he described as the great marvel of the nineteenth century. In England as well as studying railways, he had investigated the way in which the London banks operated. It was his idea that the Bank of Turin should be set up in 1847, with himself as one of its first directors.

When Charles Albert freed the press from censorship in 1847 Cavour founded his own publication *Il Risorgimento,* and used it to publicise his political ideas for the future. He welcomed the constitution ganted by Charles Albert in 1848, for one of the first proposals of *Il Risorgimento* had been for a moderate constitution. He stood for election for the first Piedmontese Parliament but failed to win a seat, though he did so a few weeks later in a by-election. Once elected he soon became well known as a non-revolutionary, liberal politician and in October 1850 was appointed Minister of Agriculture, Commerce and the Navy. He began putting into practice his economic theories and made free-trade treaties with France, Britain and Belgium. He even made one with Austria which allowed Piedmontese wines and other goods to be exported to Lombardy. The Prime Minister, D'Azeglio, did not enjoy the everyday business of government and handed over much of it to Cavour, who also became minister of finance in 1851, after he was able to obtain better terms for a government loan to build a railway than the government itself had been able to do.

By 1852 Cavour began to find himself out of sympathy with D'Azeglio's traditionally minded liberal government, and made an alliance with a moderately radical party in Parliament to form a new centre party. He was encouraged to do this by D'Azeglio's decision to reduce the freedom of the press slightly, which Cavour feared might lead on to a return to press censorship and absolute government. By the end of May 1852 Cavour's position as a minister became too difficult and he resigned from the government. He went abroad, finding time for a visit to Paris and a meeting with the President of the French Republic, Louis Napoleon. While Cavour was away a political crisis developed in Piedmont when the government decided to introduce civil marriage, allowing couples to marry without a church service. There was strong opposition from the Church. The Pope wrote a letter to the King and he put pressure on Parliament to reject the proposal. D'Azeglio resigned and suggested Cavour as his successor. Victor Emmanuel II asked Cavour to form a government on condition he dropped the civil marriage bill. Reluctantly he agreed and became Prime Minister in November 1852. He remained as Prime Minister, apart from a few months in 1859–60, until his early death in 1861. The nine years of his premiership were some of the most momentous in the history of Italy.

When Cavour became Prime Minister he had only a limited knowledge and understanding of foreign affairs. In the 1830s he had expressed a vague wish that Italy should be united and free from Austrian domination '... hoping for the soonest possible emancipation of Italy from the barbarians who oppress her' but worried because '... a crisis of at least some violence is inevitable ... I want that crisis to be as restrained as the state of things allows' and fearing that revolutionary '... movements would only make unity more difficult to achieve'. Too much should not be read into these remarks, for in the 1850s he still referred on a number of occasions to the idea of Italian unity as 'rubbish'. Probably he did not begin to see it as a realistic aim until 1859.

He soon gained the experience in foreign affairs which he lacked in 1852. Soon after he took office an international crisis led to the start of the Crimean War. Traditionally Cavour has been seen as happily joining in the war against Russia in order to gain the friendship of Britain and France and to be sure of some of the spoils as well as a seat at the eventual peace conference. Undoubtedly these things did influence his decision to join in the war. His speech to Parliament in 1855 presents his vision of a new Italy whose international reputation will be improved further by sending young men to fight in the war rather than staying at home and taking part in revolutions, plots and conspiracies which damage Italy's reputation abroad. 'The sons of Italy can fight with true valour on the field of glory ... I am sure that the laurels our soldiers will win on the battlefields of the east will do more for the future of Italy than all those who have thought to revive her with the voice and with the pen ... so that she can take her rightful place among the Great Powers'.

Some historians, however, believe that Cavour was pressured by

Britain and France into taking part in the war, partly because additional troops were needed and partly because Austria needed to be reassured that if she joined the allied armies against Russia Piedmont would not take advantage of the situation to interfere in Lombardy.

Either way, by joining in the war Cavour did achieve his aim of a seat at the peace conference held in Paris in 1856. There he was able to negotiate on almost equal terms with the Great Powers and there he also made the further acquaintance of Louis Napoleon, the future Emperor Napoleon III. They kept in touch over the next two years through members of Louis Napoleon's family until, in July 1858, Cavour was invited to a meeting at Plombières close to the Franco-Swiss border. The meeting was kept very secret – even the French Foreign Minister was not aware of what was happening and sent a note to Louis Napoleon to warn him Cavour had arrived in the town. The note reached Louis Napoleon, now Emperor Napoleon III, as he and Cavour were actually talking together. Cavour himself had been equally secretive. He had told only Victor Emmanuel and one other minister about the meeting which was beginning to look like a conspiracy.

Whose were the proposals discussed at Plombières? Napoleon had issued the invitation and organised the meeting. It might be expected that the proposals were his, but there is some evidence to suggest that Cavour took with him an outline memorandum which contained proposals very similar to what was finally agreed.

Three days later, on 24 July, Cavour sat down and wrote a very long and detailed letter to Victor Emmanuel giving his version of the discussion:

1 The ciphered letter which I sent to Your Majesty from Plombières could only give a very incomplete idea of the long conversations I had with the Emperor. I believe you will be impatient to receive an exact and detailed narration. That is what I hasten to do having just left
5 France.

As soon as I entered the Emperor's study, he raised the question which was the purpose of my journey. He began by saying that he had decided to support Piedmont with all his power in a war against Austria, provided that the war was undertaken for a non-revolutionary end
10 which could be justified in the eyes of diplomatic circles, and still more in the eyes of French and European public opinion.

Since the search for a plausible excuse presented our main problem before we could agree, I felt obliged to treat that question before any others. First I suggested that we could use the grievances occasioned by
15 Austria's bad faith in not carrying out her commercial treaty. To this the Emperor answered that a petty commercial question could not be made the occasion for a great war designed to change the map of Europe. Then I proposed to revive the objections we had made at the

Congress of Paris against the illegitimate extension of Austrian power
20 in Italy.

The Emperor did not like these pretexts. 'Besides', he added, 'inasmuch as French troops are in Rome, I can hardly demand that Austria withdraw hers from Ancona and Bologna'. This was a reasonable objection. . . .

25 My position now became embarrassing because I had no other precise proposal to make. The Emperor came to my aid and together we set ourselves to discussing each state in Italy, seeking grounds for war. It was very hard to find any.

. . . We went on to the main question: what would be the objective
30 of the war? The Emperor readily agreed that it was necessary to drive the Austrians out of Italy once and for all . . .

. . . But how was Italy to be organised after that? The valley of the Po (Piedmont), the Romagna, and the Legations (parts of the Papal States) would form a kingdom of Upper Italy under the House of Savoy (the
35 Piedmontese royal family). Rome and its immediate surroundings would be left to the Pope. The rest of the Papal States, together with Tuscany, would form a kingdom of central Italy. The Neapolitan frontier would be left unchanged. These four Italian states would form a confederation, the presidency of which would be given to the Pope to console him for
40 losing the best part of his States.

This arrangement seems to me to be fully acceptable. Your Majesty would be legal sovereign of the richest and most powerful half of Italy, and hence would in practice dominate the whole peninsula . . .

After we had settled the fate of Italy, the Emperor asked me whether
45 Your Majesty would cede Savoy and the County of Nice. I answered that Your Majesty believed in the principalities of nationalities and realised accordingly that Savoy ought to be reunited with France; and that consequently you were prepared to make this sacrifice, even though it would be extremely painful to renounce the country which
50 had been the cradle of your family and whose people had given your ancestors so many proofs of affection and devotion. The question of Nice was different, because the people of Nice, by origin, language and customs were closer to Piedmont than to France . . .

Then we proceeded to examine how the war could be won, and the
55 Emperor observed that we would have to isolate Austria so that she would be our sole opponent. That was why he deemed it so important that the grounds for war as such would not alarm the other continental powers.

. . . Unless the Emperor is deluding himself, which I am not inclined
60 to believe after all he told me, it would simply be a matter of war between France and ourselves on the one side and Austria on the other.

The Emperor nevertheless believes that, even reduced to these proportions, there remain formidable difficulties. There is no denying that
65 Austria is very strong . . .

Success will therefore require very considerable forces. The Emperor's estimate is at least 300,000 men, and I think he is right ... France would provide 200,000 men; Piedmont and the other Italian provinces the remaining 100,000.

70   Once agreed on military matters, we equally agreed on the financial question, and I must inform Your Majesty that this is what chiefly pre-occupies the Emperor. Nevertheless he is ready to provide us with whatever munitions we need, and to help us negotiate a loan in Paris.

A provisional agreement was also reached for a marriage between Victor Emmanuel's daughter, Clothilde, and one of Napoleon's cousins.

The arrangements reached at Plombières were largely incorpor-ated into a secret treaty in January 1859, although some changes were made. Cavour's objections were overcome and Nice was added to Savoy as Napoleon's proposed reward, while the idea of an Italian confederation headed by the Pope was abandoned.

To put the whole scheme into operation Cavour and Napoleon needed to provoke Austria into war. Cavour began by writing an emo-tional anti-Austrian speech for Victor Emmanuel to give at the open-ing of Parliament in January 1859 which included the words, 'We cannot be insensitive to the cry of anguish (*grido di dolore*) that comes to us from many parts of Italy'. '*Grido di dolore*' quickly became a catch phrase throughout Italy to express popular anti-Austrian feelings.

Napoleon still insisted that in any war Austria must appear as the aggressor, and this proved more difficult to arrange. In despair Napoleon even began to talk to Cavour of abandoning the idea of war, and substituting a congress of the Great Powers to settle the Italian question. Cavour was not happy with this idea and wrote to Napoleon:

1   Your Majesty knows the difficulty of our position. We concerted a plan with Your Majesty by which we would group around us all the live forces of Italy but without allowing our cause to be contaminated by any revolutionary element ... If we are now made to wait outside the
5   door while Your Majesty plays the chief role, the rest of Italy will see us as feeble and powerless. Even in Piedmont opposition will grow and and it will be hard to go on governing without exceptional measures and the use of force. I am not moved by any childish vanity or exagger-ated notion of our importance, it is just that our exclusion from a con-
10   gress would deprive us of our strength and prestige which we need for that great enterprise which is our duty and our right and which would be the glory of your reign ... Austria has misjudged you and adopted a menacing, even provocative tone. She is playing the role of an aggres-sor and this makes me hope she will before long commit one of those
15   aggressive acts which will justify your armed intervention. I hope so with all my heart.

Cavour's heartfelt wish was soon granted. In April 1859 Austria issued an ultimatum demanding that Piedmont should demobilise her army. The Austrians had already mobilised a large army in northern Italy but could not afford the expense of keeping it at the ready for very long. They dared not disband while Piedmont still had an army ready for war, and so took the dangerous step of sending the ultimatum. Cavour refused Austrian demands to demobilise and Victor Emmanuel issued a proclamation: 'People of Italy! Austria provokes Piedmont ... I fight for the right of the whole nation ... I have no other ambition than to be the first soldier of Italian independence'. Austria replied by declaring war on 29 April 1859 and the fighting began in what was to be a short, violent and terrible conflict.

3 The War of 1859

KEY ISSUES What did Piedmont gain by this war? Was it worth the losses?

The war started slowly, marked by chaos, confusion and unprepared-ness on both sides. Napoleon took several days to declare war in sup-port of his ally, and then needed further time to move his army to Italy. It travelled by train as a modern army should, but due to bad organisation, although the men arrived safely in Lombardy, their equipment and provisions did not. 'We have sent an army of 120,000 men into Italy before we have stocked up supplies' Napoleon com-plained to Paris. There were not enough tents for the men and, even worse, not enough ammunition. The only consolation was that the Austrian and Piedmontese generals were even more incompetent in moving their men so that it was some time before fighting could actu-ally begin.

Lombardy was quickly overrun by a combined French and Piedmontese army and the Austrian army was heavily defeated at Magenta on 4 June and at Solferino on 24 June. The carnage at both battles and on both sides was horrific. The Austrian Emperor, Victor Emmanuel and Napoleon, all present as spectators, were deeply shocked. Napoleon offered his personal linen to be torn up as band-ages for his men, but this gesture hardly compensated the wounded for the fact that the official bandages, along with the medical and other supplies, did not arrive until after the war was over. For most of them this was in any case too late. There was no provision for those who lay, often terribly maimed, on the battlefield for hours without help and with death as their only hope, as the local peasantry stripped the boots from the bodies of dead and dying alike.

The only good thing to come out of this useless slaughter was the arrival on the battlefield of the Swiss journalist Henry Dunant, whose reports of the horrors which he saw led eventually to the formation of the Red Cross organisation.

The war was mercifully short – only seven weeks – because on 11 July 1859 Napoleon suddenly made a truce with Austria. In August he met Franz Joseph, the young Austrian Emperor, at Villafranca and agreed an armistice, the terms of which were accepted by Victor Emmanuel without consulting Cavour. By it, Piedmont received Lombardy, although to allow Austria to save face, it was first ceded (officially handed over) to France and then passed by Napoleon to Victor Emmanuel. Austria still kept Venetia and therefore remained a powerful influence in Italy.

As he had not fulfilled all his promises made at Plombières, Napoleon could not demand that Savoy and Nice should be immediately handed over to France. They remained, for the time being, part of Italy.

Why did Napoleon make his sudden and unexpected truce with Austria in July and after his meeting with Franz Joseph, the young Austrian Emperor, agree, without consulting Cavour, the armistice of Villafranca in August 1859? There are many possibilities but no certainties about why he behaved as he did.

As a military leader Napoleon was full of good intentions, but incompetent. The battles of Magenta and Solferino with their great loss of life affected him severely. He seems to have suffered from some sort of nervous breakdown, perhaps arising from a sense of guilt for having engineered the war, in the days which followed. He may have felt that by bringing the war to an early end he could at least prevent another disaster on the scale of Solferino. The Austrians had withdrawn into their stronghold of the 'quadrilateral', a group of four heavily defended fortresses near the Austrian border. There was no hope that what was left of the French and Piedmontese armies could possibly breach the Austrian defences. Reinforcements would be needed and obtaining these would take time. There was danger too that Prussia, already mobilising along the Rhine frontier, might take advantage of Napoleon's absence to attack France. Alternatively, Prussia might decide to come to the aid of Austria if the war were allowed to continue and a combined Prusso-Austrian army would be invincible. In France itself, there was growing criticism of the whole Italian adventure, and Napoleon was becoming increasingly suspicious of Cavour's activities. In Tuscany the Grand Duke had left his Duchy and gone to Vienna, and a provisional government had announced it wished Tuscany to be united with Piedmont. Revolution spread to Modena and Parma where Piedmontese armies moved in and took over, setting up provisional governments, while Cavour's agents were known to be encouraging revolution in the Papal States. Everywhere it seemed to Napoleon that Piedmont was trying to gain more territory and more power than had been agreed at Plombières as her share of the spoils.

Everything though was not going smoothly for Cavour. Victor Emmanuel had been persuaded to accept the terms of the armistice of Villafranca. By it, the rulers of Tuscany, Modena and Parma were to be restored to their Duchies even though it was not made clear how this was to be done and did not in fact come to pass. Cavour, who had not been consulted, was furious. In a hysterical interview with Victor Emmanuel he resigned as Prime Minister. While he was out of office for the next nine months, the future of central Italy was decided. In Tuscany, a carefully rigged assembly voted unanimously in August for union with Piedmont. So too did Modena and the Romagna in the Papal States. Because of the expected opposition of Napoleon, these unions were not immediately put into effect. Instead, provisional, pro-Piedmontese governments were left in control in each of the states.

The Armistice of Villafranca developed into a peace conference held in Zurich in November and this time Piedmont was invited to send representatives. In the Peace of Prague which followed, the handing over by Austria of Lombardy first to France and then by Napoleon to Piedmont was confirmed; the problems of central Italy were shelved, to be dealt with by one of Napoleon's favourite methods, a Congress. This never took place. A document leaked by the French goverment suggesting that the Pope should not revive the idea of a confederation under his presidency, but resign himself to the loss of most of the Papal States, led to the Pope's anger and a refusal by the Austrian government to take part in any Congress which followed that line.

Partly as a result of this and partly because of pressure by the British government, Napoleon had become more sympathetic to the idea of the union of north and central Italy into a single state under the control of Piedmont by the time Cavour returned to power as Prime Minister in early 1860. By then Cavour realised that the one way to restore good relations with Napoleon was to arrange for Nice and Savoy to be handed over to him without further delay.

In mid-March 1860 in Tuscany and in the new state of Emilia (made up of the Duchies of Modena and Parma together with the Romagna) the population voted for union with Piedmont. This was in fact a foregone conclusion after the provisional governments had carried out very extensive propaganda campaigns. In Emilia 427,512 voted for union with Piedmont and 756 voted against. In Turin decrees were published declaring Tuscany and Emilia part of the Kingdom of Piedmont.

A secret treaty between Victor Emmanuel and Napoleon in March transferred Savoy and Nice to France, subject to the results of a popular vote in both places. These votes were taken in April and again huge majorities voted in favour of union. The result in French-speaking Savoy was not unexpected, but in Nice which was Italian-speaking, the results were suspicious – 24,484 in favour and only 160 against. The presence of a French army in Nice on its way home from Lombardy at the time may have had something to do with the result. Among those who questioned the accuracy of the results was Garibaldi who had been born in Nice and was one of its elected representatives in the Piedmontese parliament. He was preparing a military expedition to prevent Nice being taken over by France when he was diverted by an outbreak of revolution in southern Italy on the island of Sicily.

4 Cavour and Garibaldi

> **KEY ISSUES** Why did Cavour and Garibaldi not get on with each other? How did their disagreements affect the political/military situation in 1859–60?

Historians have argued for a long time about the motives of Cavour and Garibaldi and the relations between the two men. In every way they were a contrast. Cavour was the nobleman, well-educated, intelligent, cool, calm and collected, the fat little politician and diplomat. Garibaldi was the rough, ill-educated soldier and leader of men. Ready to take chances at any time, passionate and charismatic, his ideas were simple and straightforward. He did not allow them to get in the way of action. He had come under the influence of Mazzini in 1831 and, although he afterwards abandoned republican ideals, becoming instead a monarchist and following Victor Emmanuel II, he always retained his nationalist beliefs and continued to fight for an independent and united Italy. All his actions were aimed at driving out Austria, the foreigner, from Italian soil and establishing an Italian kingdom under the rule of Piedmont. These aims became an obsession which dominated his life and dictated his every action.

How far Cavour's aims were similar is open to question. He had written in the 1830s about the possibility of a united Italy, but the first sign that he was thinking seriously how to achieve it was the letter which he wrote to Victor Emmanuel after the meeting at Plombières with Napoleon, though even in this he does not seem to be fully committed to the idea of a united Italy.

Cavour was realistic enough to know that '*Italia fara da se*' (Italy will make herself by herself) as Charles Albert had hoped and expected, was an impossible aim. There was no hope of Piedmont being able to expel Austria from northern Italy without outside help, and the only available souce of help was Napoleon and the French army. Cavour reasoned that France would be prepared to help, at least up to a point, in return for Nice and Savoy, but he also realised that Napoleon would not agree to unlimited expansion of Piedmont and would not wish Piedmont to become the leader of a united Italy because an Italy of separate states could be useful to France in any conflict with Austria. A united Italy on the other hand might become a possible threat to France herself. For this reason France had at first opposed the take-over by Piedmont of Tuscany and Emilia, and not until Napoleon changed his mind and agreed to Piedmont's takeover of these two states in early 1860, did Cavour see the unification of Italy as a real possibility.

Even then he does not seem to have been convinced that a totally united Italy was either possible or desirable. Piedmont had gained control over northern Italy by diplomacy and limited war; anything more in the way of territorial gains might need a major civil war, and this was not what Cavour wanted. For him it was time to stop. Not so for Garibaldi.

Garibaldi wanted Rome and Venetia, Naples and Sicily, as part of a united Italy and wanted them at once. He planned a military expedition to unite southern Italy with Piedmont by revolution. His expedition and its results are dealt with in the next chapter (pages 69–73)

It is difficult to know what Cavour thought of Garibaldi's plan. Some historians believe that Cavour pretended to stop Garibaldi while secretly supporting him. This may have been because he thought of Garibaldi as an ally or because he intended from the start to use Garibaldi for his own purposes. Cavour was anyway in a difficult situation in Piedmont where elections were taking place. He feared that open opposition to Garibaldi might lead to loss of popular support for the government.

He needed to be careful: ' I omitted nothing to persuade Garibaldi to drop his mad scheme', wrote Cavour just before Garibaldi set out. When it became clear in early August that the expedition had been successful, Cavour changed his public announcement to one of admiration: 'Garibaldi has rendered Italy the greatest services that a man could give her; he has given Italians confidence in themselves; he has proved to Europe that Italians know how to fight and die on the battlefield to reconquer a fatherland'. By this time it is clear that even Cavour was talking of 'Italy' as though the country had already been unified – a great step forward for the politically cautious Cavour to make. He seems to have seen unification as now inevitable, whether he agreed with it or not.

Other historians see Cavour as Garibaldi's enemy, opposed to his plans for unification, and while pretending to help the expedition, secretly working to make sure that it would fail. They believe that he disliked the whole idea of Garibaldi's expedition to attack Sicily and Naples. There was in fact a real chance that the expedition would fail as others had done in the past, and Cavour as Prime Minister would be held responsible for the defeat and for loss of life.

On a personal level Cavour disliked Garibaldi. He thought that he was stupid and probably untrustworthy. Garibaldi had been a republican and had only lately become a royalist. Cavour remained unsure whether this change of heart was genuine, and continued to suspect Garibaldi of being a Mazzinian and to fear that if he were successful in southern Italy he might demand a republican Italy. At best this demand would lead to a divided country with a republic in the south and a monarchy in the north.

When, against all expectations, Garibaldi's expedition to Sicily proved successful, Cavour decided that Piedmont should take over Sicily immediately. There were difficulties in doing this, for Sicily was part of the Kingdom of Naples and could not just be absorbed by Piedmont. While the Sicilians wanted independence from Naples they certainly did not want to replace Naples with Piedmont.

Cavour was still considering how to act, when news came that Garibaldi was marching north through Naples towards Rome.

Cavour may have thought that France and perhaps also Austria would intervene if Garibaldi's army entered the Papal States. France had kept a garrison in Rome since the days of the Roman Republic. Any attack on the city would lead to conflict. Cavour was also worried about the growing popularity of Garibaldi not only in Sicily, but also in Piedmont. It was possible that he might lead a revolution and take over Piedmont.

If that happened he would probably end by taking over the whole of Italy. Cavour had to act. He decided to organise an invasion of the Papal States from the north to block Garibaldi's army, which was invading from the south, before he could reach Rome and the Pope. The invading Piedmontese troops were not well received in the Papal States and met considerable opposition from the civilian population on their way south to stop Garibaldi's army. With the meeting of the two armies all of southern and central Italy came under the effective control of Piedmont. Cavour's gamble on invading the Papal States had paid off, and made the unification of Italy under the leadership of Piedmont and the government of Victor Emmanuel a reality.

Cavour arranged for the people of Naples and afterwards of Sicily to vote whether or not there should be a united Italy under Victor Emmanuel and asked '*Italia una Vittorio Emmanuele?* Organising the voting was particularly difficult in Sicily where most of population was illiterate and did not speak or understand the Italian of the north. Difficulties were allegedly overcome by providing each voter with two voting slips, one saying 'yes' the other 'no', and by having two ballot boxes similarly marked. Unfortunately even those who could read had no idea who or what Vittorio Emmanuele was. Union with Piedmont was not mentioned. Even the word 'Italia' which had been Garibaldi's slogan during the fighting merely confused Sicilians further. Following careful preparations by Piedmontese officials there was, however, an overwhelming vote in favour of union.

Voting also took place in November 1860 in the eastern and central parts of the Papal States occupied by Piedmont, and again enormous numbers voted for union with Piedmont.

In March 1861 the Kingdom of Italy was proclaimed, with Victor Emmanuel II as King of Italy. Not quite all of the peninsula was then part of the new Kingdom: the Patrimony of St. Peter, the area around Rome, remained under the control of the Pope and in French occupation until 1870; Venetia remained in Austrian hands until 1866. Everywhere else unification was complete and under the control of Piedmont.

Cavour did not live to see a fully united and independent Italy. He died in March 1861 from 'a fever'.

References

Vyvyen Brendon, *The Making of Modern Italy,* (Hodder & Stoughton, 1998)

Summary Diagram

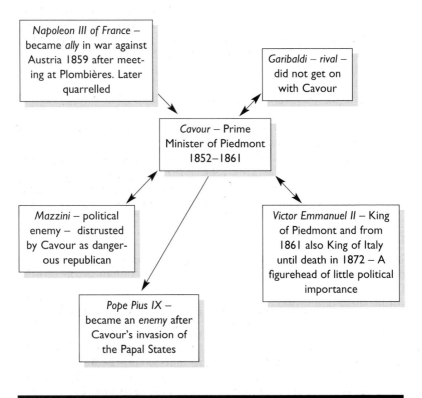

Napoleon III of France — became *ally* in war against Austria 1859 after meeting at Plombières. Later quarrelled

Garibaldi — *rival* — did not get on with Cavour

Cavour — Prime Minister of Piedmont 1852–1861

Mazzini — political enemy — distrusted by Cavour as dangerous republican

Victor Emmanuel II — King of Piedmont and from 1861 also King of Italy until death in 1872 — A figurehead of little political importance

Pope Pius IX — became an *enemy* after Cavour's invasion of the Papal States

Working on Chapter 3

Two important topics are covered in Chapter 3. The first relates to the stages by which Piedmont emerged as the dominant state in Italy and the only state strong enough to lead the struggle for the unification and independence of the country. The second considers the part played in these events by Count Camillo Cavour. As you read through the chapter again, make a point of identifying the factors that are central to these topics. Remember most syllabuses requiring an in-depth study of the *Risorgimento* cover the years 1848 to 1870–71 and so it is obviously best to concentrate on that period. In your assessment of Cavour it will be helpful to make notes that cover the politician's career from two points of view. Firstly consider his importance as a Piedmontese statesman and his contribution towards the modernisation and democratisation of his country. Secondly make an estimate of his importance as an Italian nationalist and his role in bringing about the unification of his country. You might also consider the real aims of Cavour. Did he simply work to extend the influence of Piedmont and to ensure that Victor Emmanuel II became the first ruler of a united Italy, or was he truly a nationalist and patriot who placed the need to create an independent Italian state above all else? Once you have studied Chapter 4, you will be in a position to compare the achievements of Cavour with those of the other great champion of Italian nationhood, Giuseppe Garibaldi.

Answering structured questions on Chapter 3

1. a) Explain the meanings of the following terms used in the Articles of the *Statuto* (see pages 41–2):
(i) inviolable, (ii) executive power, (iii) promulgates laws, (iv) commute punishment, (v) convokes. (5 × 2 = *10 marks*)
b) For what reasons did Charles Albert (i) declare war on Austria in 1848 and (ii) seek an armistice with Austria the following year? (2 × 5 = *10 marks*)

Answering source-based questions on Chapter 3

Read the letter written by Cavour to Victor Emmanuel concerning his meeting with the Emperor Napoleon III, at Plombières in 1858 (pages 47–49) and then answer the following questions:

1. a) (i) What did Napoleon III mean by 'which could be justified in the eyes of diplomatic circles' (page 47 line 10)? (*2 marks*)
(ii) What did Cavour mean by 'I answered that Your Majesty believed in the principalities of nationalities' (page 48 line 45–6)? (*2 marks*)
b) What information can be inferred from the source about Cavour's enthusiasm to involve France in a war with Austria? (*6 marks*)
c) How useful is the source to an understanding of the background to the Franco-Piedmontese war with Austria of 1859? In your answer

use relevant background knowledge as well as information derived from the source. (*10 marks*)

Answering essay questions on Chapter 3

1 To what extent had the obstacles to Italian unity been overcome by 1861? (*25 marks*)
2 How important was the contribution of Cavour to Italian unification? (*25 marks*)

Before attempting question 1, it is necessary to read again details of the obstacles to Italian unification outlined in Chapter 2. Remember it is not sufficient to describe the nature of these obstacles. To obtain the higher marks, it is necessary to examine the extent to which these obstacles had been overcome by 1861. You will need to explain what had been achieved and what remained to be done before the process of unification could be considered complete. Similarly in question 2, it is not sufficient to write a factual account of the career of Cavour prior to his death in 1861. Examiners will be impressed by answers that assess the importance of Cavour's contribution. Does the credit for the achievement of Italian unification accrue to him alone? How valuable was Cavour's contribution compared with that of others?

Garibaldi and Italy

POINTS TO CONSIDER

This chapter is quite straightforward. The first part deals with Garibaldi's early life and should help you decide what sort of a person he was and why he behaved as he did. The later part of the chapter deals with his conquest of Sicily and Naples in 1860 and its importance for the unification of Italy. It also considers Garibaldi's achievements and failures and suggests reasons why he and Cavour disagreed.

KEY DATES

1807 Garibaldi born in Nice, at that time part of France.

1815 Nice returned to Piedmont in the Vienna Settlement.

1831 Garibaldi met Mazzini by chance in Marseilles and became a republican.

1833 Garibaldi involved in Mazzini's unsuccessful revolutionary plot in Piedmont. Escaped to South America where he founded the Legion.

1848 Hearing rumours of revolution returned to Italy and became the greatest guerrilla leader of the nineteenth century with Legion of 5000 men. Offered services to Charles Albert and became a royalist.

1849 Fought bravely but unsuccessfully in defence of the Roman Republic. Escaped to North America.

1859 Invited back to Italy by Cavour and became wholehearted supporter of Victor Emmanuel II.

1860 Took 'The Thousand' to Sicily – overran southern Italy – disagreed with Cavour.

1862 and 1867 Attempted unsuccessfully to take Rome.

1870 Offered services to France but was declined. Retired to the island of Caprera.

1882 Death of Garibaldi aged 75.

1 Garibaldi 1807–48

Today, in Britain, the name Garibaldi is hardly remembered at all, except perhaps as the name of a currant biscuit, but in Victorian England it was a name to conjure with. He was the swashbuckling adventurer, the national patriot, the leader of men, who had struck a blow for the freedom of his country. On a state visit to Britain towards the end of the nineteenth century he was greeted with enormous enthusiasm by the largest crowds seen in London for many a long day, all of whom wanted to touch his hand as he rode in a state procession. During the drive he was greeted with a great deal more applause and excitement than Queen Victoria who accompanied him, very much to her annoyance. Soon afterwards his visit was cut short – it is generally believed on royal orders. After all, competition with the sovereign could not be allowed, especially from a foreigner. He was sent home to Italy.

Garibaldi's life by any standards was colourful and dramatic. He described it as having been tempestuous, made up of good and evil, and this was true. He was born a French citizen in Nice in 1807, but was only eight years old when Nice became part of Piedmont after the Congress of Vienna in 1815. In any case both his parents were Italian and he always thought of himself as Italian. His father was a sailor and despite his family's wishes that he should enter the church and become a priest, Garibaldi followed his father and joined the merchant navy. It was as a result of this that a chance encounter in Marseilles in 1831 brought him into contact with Mazzini and altered his life for ever.

Mazzini, the founder of 'Young Italy', believed that Italy should be free, independent and united, not as a monarchy but as a republic where the people should have a say in government. Mazzini's greatest gift was probably to inspire revolutionary leaders with nationalist fervour and patriotic enthusiasm, and the greatest of his disciples was Garibaldi. Garibaldi was quickly converted to the dream of a united Italy, joined the 'Young Italy' movement, and in 1833 became involved in Mazzini's revolutionary plot in Piedmont. The plot, intended to start a mutiny in the army and navy, went wrong, and Garibaldi was among those sentenced to death for their part in it.

Fortunately for Garibaldi he had already left the country before the trial began and the sentence could not be carried out. Signing on as second mate he sailed for South America and settled in Rio de Janeiro. There he found that a branch of 'Young Italy' was already established. He joined it and quickly became involved in revolutionary plans. Planning though was not enough for him. He wanted action and for a while he became a pirate preying on the shipping of the New World, and then joined a rebel army in Brazil. In between campaigns he found time to fall in love and run away with a fisherman's wife who became his devoted, insanely jealous companion for the next ten years.

After six years of fighting, Garibaldi retired to Montevideo in Uruguay and a humdrum life as a commercial traveller selling spaghetti. He quickly became bored by this and joined the army defending Uruguay against an Argentinian takeover. He raised an Italian legion of guerrilla fighters which fought with much bravery if little skill, and was largely responsible for the final Uruguayan victory. It was during this time that Garibaldi's men wore the famous red shirt for the first time. Originally modelled on the South American poncho, a circular cape-like garment with no sleeves or fastenings, and merely a hole for the head, Garibaldi had seen it being worn by the local slaughtermen. It was cheap and easy to make and being red in colour did not show the blood, either of cattle or men. Later, inspired by the uniform of the New York Fire Brigade, Garibaldi introduced sleeves, and then brass buttons, making the whole design much more like that of a shirt. After his return with his legionaries to Italy, the manufacture of these shirts was willingly undertaken by young seamstresses sympathetic to his cause.

The Seamstresses of the Red Shirts (1863) by Odoardo Borrani.

A lithograph of Garibaldi from 1850
likening him to Christ.

A portrait of Garibaldi by Altamura Saverio.

Instead of the red shirt, Garibaldi himself sometimes wore a white poncho, a relic of his South American days, and his portraits show him with a circle-brimmed hat tipped over one eye. His shapeless trousers were homemade by himself, but as he never mastered button holes they had to be tied up with laces. He preferred a simple life and ate little. Rather rough in manner, he was generally good humoured, but could be ruthless and determined. His main interests were fighting and women. He collected a large number of women over the years in addition to the three he married.

Scandal and gossip followed him, but could not hide his success as a guerrilla leader nor his devotion to the cause of Italian unity.

On his return to Italy he was to inspire great devotion from his men, and a near-religious adoration from ordinary people. Street songs, ballads and popular prints of the time show him as semi-divine: in effect a local patron saint, his portrait displayed in a place of honour next to that of the Madonna in Italian homes. His charisma was overwhelming.

2 Garibaldi and the Revolutions of 1848–9

> **KEY ISSUES** How important was the part played by Garibaldi in the revolutions of 1848–9? Why did the Roman Republic last such a short time?

In 1848, hearing rumours of a revolution in Italy Garibaldi decided to return home, accompanied by sixty of his men and a number of out-of-date weapons.

When he arrived in Nice, Garibaldi immediately offered his military services to Charles Albert, King of Piedmont. This was a surprising thing for him, as a declared republican, to do. Charles Albert must have been surprised also. The King mistrusted the offer and refused to see Garibaldi, sending him instead to the War Minister, who also refused the offer. Nobody it seemed trusted or wanted the Garibaldini and their leader, until the Revolutionary government of Milan in Lombardy asked for their help to drive out the Austrians. Extra recruits were enlisted and an army of 5000 men was formed, but before it could go into action the news came that Charles Albert's Piedmontese army had been defeated at Custoza. On hearing this most of the legionaries deserted. The few who remained fought a number of skirmishes, and scored several minor successes against the Austrians. Later, an Austrian general remarked that the one man who could have helped the Italians win the 1848 war, was the one man they turned their backs on.

Why did Garibaldi offer his services to Charles Albert? It marked a turning point in his life, changing him from a republican to a royalist. He seems to have believed that only Charles Albert as King of Piedmont had the resources to defeat the Austrians and unite Italy. So he abandoned the republican beliefs he had learnt from Mazzini, (although he kept his opposition to the Catholic Church), in the cause of Italian unity. Garibaldi's unexpected change of heart seems to have been quite sincere. 'I was a republican, but when I discovered that Charles Albert had made himself champion of Italy I swore to obey him and faithfully to follow his banner'. Mazzini was deeply hurt at what he saw as a betrayal of the revolutionary cause by Garibaldi. Even Charles Albert was not wholehearted in welcoming his new follower, but Garibaldi, always single-minded in his devotion to the cause of Italian unity, could see no way of achieving it except by attaching himself to Charles Albert and afterwards to his successors. It brought to an end the good relationship he had always had with Mazzini. They parted company politically, although both were to work together in the heroic defence of the Roman Republic.

a) The Roman Republic 1849

KEY ISSUE Why was Rome so important to both Italians and the French?

The Roman Republic was declared in February 1849 after the Pope had refused to make political changes in the government of Rome and was forced to escape from the city to safety in southern Italy. The Republic was shortlived, only surviving for four months. It was led by a Triumvirate, a government of three men, headed by Mazzini (see the illustration on page 65). Under his influence Rome had never been better governed.

Garibaldi and the legionaries arrived in Rome as the city prepared, in Mazzini's words, 'to resist, resist whatever the cost, in the name of independence, in the name of honour and the right of all states, great or small, weak or strong, to govern themselves'.

Garibaldi appeared a striking figure, patrolling the city defences, according to a Dutch artist who saw him in Rome in 1849:

1 Garibaldi entered through the gate. It was the first time I had seen the man whose name everyone in Rome knew and in whom many had placed their hopes. Of middle height, well built, broad shouldered, his square chest gives a sense of power – he stood there before us; his blue
5 eyes verging on violet, surveyed in one glance the entire group. Those eyes had something remarkable ... they contrasted curiously with those dark sparkling eyes of his Italian soldiers, and his light chestnut brown hair, which fell loosely over his shoulders, contrasting with their shining black curls. His face was burnt red with the sun and his face covered
10 with freckles. A heavy moustache and a light blonde beard ending in two

Lithograph of Mazzini with the other two triumvirs of the Roman Republic, Carlo Armellini and Aurelio Saffi.

points gave a military expression to his face. Most striking was his broad nose which has caused him to be given the name of *Leone* and indeed made one think of a lion; a resemblance which according to his soldiers was still more conspicuous in a fight when his eyes short forth flames
15 and his hair waved as a mane upon his head.

He was dressed in a red tunic and on his head was a little black felt, sugar loaf hat, with two black ostrich feathers. In his left hand he had a sabre and a cartridge bag hung from his left shoulder.

The Pope had appealed to Austria and Spain for help, but it was not from these Catholic monarchies which might have been expected to come to the aid of the Pope, but from the President of another Republic, Louis Napoleon of France that help came. A French army arrived at the gates of Rome, but was driven back. During a temporary truce French reinforcements arrived and Garibaldi drove off a Neapolitan attack. The end came quickly as the defenders, heavily outnumbered, fought bravely but in vain.

On 3 July 1849 the Roman Republic fell to the soldiers of the French Republic. On the day before, Garibaldi had made a theatrical entry into the Assembly meeting with a sword so bent and battered from hand to hand fighting that it would no longer fit in its scabbard. He announced that further resistance was useless. The Assembly appointed him Dictator of Rome to make what arrangements he thought necessary. He outlined possible action to the Assembly: to surrender the city (impossible), to continue to fight inside the city (suicidal in view of the greatly reinforced French army now numbering 20,000 men, twice the size of the defending army), or to withdraw as many men as possible towards Venetia, where the Republic there was still holding out against a besieging Austrian army (the only acceptable option).

Garibaldi appealed to the crowd in the Piazza of St. Peter:

1 Fortune who betrays us today will smile on us tomorrow. I am going out from Rome. Let those who wish to continue the war against the stranger, come with me. I offer neither pay, nor quarters, nor provisions; I offer hunger, thirst, forced marches, battles and death. Let him
5 who loves his country in his heart and not with his lips only, follow me.

He collected nearly 5000 men, almost all his soldiers who had not been killed in the defence of Rome, and began a forced march towards the Adriatic coast. This march became one of the epic tales of the *Risorgimento*. Over 800 kilometres of mountainous country, a shortage of food and water, and pursuit by enemy troops all took their toll. Only 1500 men reached the coast. Garibaldi's wife, who had accompanied him everywhere during the past ten years and often fought alongside him, died on the way and he was unable to stop long enough to bury her. Many of the Garibaldini were killed or captured or deserted to become bandits. Garibaldi himself escaped to Genoa where he was arrested but later freed on condition that he left Italy at once. His career as a revolutionary soldier-hero seemed to be over, the drama played out, the legend finished as he once again set sail across the Atlantic, this time to North America.

3 Garibaldi 1849–59

> **KEY ISSUE** What happened during these years to cause friction between Cavour and Garibaldi?

In the United States he found what employment he could, eventually going back again to sea as master of a ship on the China run, until he inherited some money from his brother. He used this to buy half of the small island of Caprera off the coast of the island of Sardinia. There he took up farming but was able to keep in touch with events in Italy through the National Society, which was now working for the unification of Italy not as a republic but as a monarchy under the leadership of the King of Piedmont.

In the ten years since Garibaldi had left Italy there had been many changes. The situation in Piedmont itself was greatly altered. Charles Albert had been succeeded by his son, Victor Emmanuel, who was pleasant, easy-going, lazy, and not unlike Garibaldi in his down-to-earth honest approach. He was, however, much more politically able than he appeared and managed somehow to keep on good terms with both Cavour and Garibaldi. He inspired great loyalty from the latter, though there is some doubt about how far Victor Emmanuel felt any loyalty towards Garibaldi.

Cavour was by now chief minister, but his views on the need for Italian unity were still unclear.

After Cavour's meeting with Napoleon III at Plombières, Cavour sent an invitation to Garibaldi through the National Society to visit Turin. There at a meeting with Cavour and Victor Emmanuel he was given details of the plans for forcing war on Austria in the spring of 1859. Garibaldi offered to recruit and train volunteers. He had now completely abandoned Mazzini and thrown in his lot with Victor Emmanuel.

In the spring of 1859 the war against Austria, known in Italy as the Second War of Independence, began (see Chapter 5 for details of the war). The armies of Piedmont and France were badly organised, the Austrians even more so and French and Piedmontese troops were able to conquer Lombardy. Garibaldi's men played an important part in the fighting in northern Italy and he himself was presented by Victor Emmanuel with the Gold Medal for valour, the highest military decoration in Piedmont.

As part of the agreement with Napoleon for French support during the war, Nice and Savoy had to be ceded (given up) to France. The handing over of Nice, the city of his birth, was a bitter blow to Garibaldi and embittered his relations with Cavour until the latter's death in 1861. Victor Emmanuel was now king of all northern Italy except Venetia. To Garibaldi it seemed as if the moment of independence was at hand and he began collecting money to buy a million rifles for use when that moment actually arrived. It was, indeed, not far off and Garibaldi was to help in bringing it into being.

4 Garibaldi and 'The Thousand'

KEY ISSUES Cavour had serious doubts about the expedition. What were they? How did they affect his relationship with Garibaldi?

In April 1860 a revolt started in Palermo in Sicily against the King of Naples. It was almost certainly organised by followers of Mazzini and supported by the National Society with its contacts throughout Italy. At the time Garibaldi was working on an armed expedition to recover Nice from France. This would include blowing up the ballot boxes to be used by those voting on whether Nice should remain Italian or again become French. He was, fortunately for everyone, diverted from this plan by news of the revolt in Sicily.

He began to collect more volunteers and by early May 1860 had a force of about 1200, mostly very young men, who were known as 'The Thousand'. He also had with him his current mistress and a thousand rifles, but no ammunition, aboard two old paddle steamers in the port of Genoa, ready to sail in the name of 'Italy and Victor Emmanuel' in support of a revolt which it was already known had failed. However, other revolts in Sicily were still going on.

Common sense suggested the expedition was unlikely to be successful. It had been put together too quickly, the number of men was too small and their resources too poor, while it was known that the enemy forces were large. It was also known that previous expeditions of this kind had failed, including a much larger one in 1857. Garibaldi was a brilliant leader of men but had no understanding of military tactics, and Cavour was not convinced that an attempt to conquer Sicily was a good idea, and might in any case be beyond Garibaldi's capabilities to carry out. In addition, in Cavour's opinion, Sicily like the rest of the south was too poor and backward to be ready for a takeover by Piedmont. Therefore, he refused Garibaldi's request for arms and equipment for the expedition, and made it clear that it went without Piedmontese official support.

Some later reports suggested that Cavour tried to persuade Victor Emmanuel to arrest Garibaldi, but was too late. The expedition had already sailed.

In a note to his confidential agent in Paris, Cavour made it clear that he had 'made every effort to persuade Garibaldi to drop his mad scheme', but could 'not stop him going, for force would have been necessary', which would have led to 'immense unpopularity had Garibaldi been prevented'. In the end he comforted himself with the idea that if the expedition failed he would be rid of Garibaldi, 'a troublesome fellow', and if it succeeded 'Italy would get some benefit from it'.

Within a week Garibaldi had landed unopposed at Marsala in Sicily. From here he and his men advanced on Palermo, the island capital, gathering support on the way and defeating a Neapolitan army in a hand-to-hand battle. In pouring rain 'The Thousand' now numbering nearer 3000 reached Palermo at the end of May and found 20,000 enemy troops waiting for them. One of The Thousand described the battle for Palermo:

> There was no sign of any local uprising until quite late in the day. We were on our own, 800 of us at most, spread out over an area as large as Milan. It was impossible to expect any planning let alone any orders, but somehow we managed to take the city against 25,000 well-armed
> 5 and well-mounted regular soldiers. We were real ragamuffins ... we ran in ones and twos through alleys and squares chasing Neapolitans and trying to stir up the Palmeritans. The Neapolitans were too busy run-

ning away and the Palmeritans in taking refuge from the gunfire ... when
Palermo finally fell it was all our doing, ours alone. Garibaldi showed the
10 height of courage and we too were heroes just because we believed in
what was impossible.

Garibaldi quickly took possession of Palermo, the garrison withdrew to Naples and the island of Sicily was his. His success outside
Palermo was helped by the fact that an earlier revolt had left much of
the island in a state of chaos, with bands of peasants roaming about
looking for revenge against Neapolitan troops and oppressive landlords. Therefore, the speed of Garibaldi's success was partly due to his
dashing and bold style of leadership and partly due to the caution of
Neapolitan officers worried about possible ambushes of their men by
Sicilian bandits and dispossessed peasants.

Garibaldi appointed himself as 'Dictator' of Sicily and at first was
sympathetic to the aims of the peasant revolt. He abolished the tax collected on corn being milled into flour which was a standing grievance
of the peasants, and won their support by promising a redistribution
of land. Soon though he changed sides and suppressed a number of
new peasant revolts. By this he lost the support of the peasants but
won that of the landlords whose help he needed to restore law and
order. He needed peace and stability in the island in order to be able
to use Sicily as a jumping-off ground for an attack on the mainland of
Italy and the next stage of unification. His obsession with a united Italy
had led him to betray Mazzini's teaching about the importance of
supporting the underprivileged.

A report to Cavour on the situation in Sicily in June 1860 showed
all was not well:

1 Garibaldi is greatly beloved. But no one believes him capable of running
a government... No one wishes to wound him, but all are determined
not to tolerate a government which is no government... He is troubled, irritated and weary beyond belief and his conversation clearly
5 shows that the cares of government are crushing and overwhelming
him.

As part of his law and order campaign Garibaldi introduced
Piedmontese laws into Sicily as a preparation for annexation by
Piedmont, but for the moment refused to hand over Sicily to Victor
Emmanuel. He was afraid that if he did so Cavour would stop him
using Sicily as a base for the campaign against Naples. Cavour was
undoubtedly surprised at Garibaldi's success in Sicily and probably
displeased at the public acclaim. Garibaldi was too much in the lime-
light and likely to take too much of the credit to himself for uniting
Italy if he was allowed to continue unchecked. Cavour would have
preferred things done more quietly, more constitutionally and with
the credit going to Piedmont and Victor Emmanuel. He wrote in a
letter to the Piedmontese ambassador in London:

12 July Garibaldi has become intoxicated by his success and by the praise showered on him from all over Europe. He is planning the wildest, not to say absurdest schemes. As he remains loyal to Victor Emmanuel he will not help Mazzini or republicanism, but he feels it is his duty to liberate all Italy, stage by stage, before handing it over to the King... He wants to raise an army to conquer first Naples, then Rome and in the end Venice.

A month later he wrote:

9 August Garibaldi has done the greatest service that a man can do; he has given the Italians self-confidence; he has proved to Europe that Italians can fight and die in battle to reconquer a fatherland... If in spite of all our efforts he should liberate southern Italy as he liberated Sicily, we would have no choice but to go along with him and wholeheartedly.

Cavour tried to arrange a revolution in Naples in favour of Victor Emmanuel before Garibaldi could get there. Orders were given to stop Garibaldi and his men from crossing the Straits of Messina to the mainland. Victor Emmanuel sent a letter to Garibaldi ordering him not to cross, following it up with another letter telling him not to take any notice of the first one. It is doubtful if Garibaldi received these letters or even whether they were ever delivered. It looks as if Victor Emmanuel was trying to be on the sides of Garibaldi and Cavour at the same time.

Typically Garibaldi solved his problems by speedy action. Dodging the ships sent to stop him he ferried his men across the Straits to Calabria. Although heavily outnumbered he fought his way north towards the city of Naples. When he heard that the King of Naples had left the city, he accepted its surrender, arriving there in advance of his troops, by train and almost alone. For the next two months he ruled as dictator over the Kingdom of Naples, unable to advance any further because the way was barred by a Neapolitan military stronghold in the north. Garibaldi's plan to move ahead and on through the Papal States to Rome and so complete the geographical unification of Italy was held up long enough for Cavour to act.

Cavour did not much like what Garibaldi had been doing in Sicily and Naples. He believed that an attack on Rome, such as Garibaldi planned, would lead to difficulties, especially with France. Napoleon III was already upset because two months earlier on his way south, Garibaldi had landed a small force in the Papal States. That expedition fizzled out, but the warning of more to come was clear. The danger was that France and the rest of Catholic Europe would act if the Pope or the city of Rome were threatened.

Cavour was aware that many of the men who had joined Garibaldi (the Garibaldini now numbered about 60,000 men) were Mazzinians. This meant that they were opposed to the Church and its teachings and would be only too glad to join in an attack on Rome. They were also republicans and this posed another threat. It could mean that if they won control the whole nationalist leadership would slip away from Piedmont and Victor Emmanuel, and become again republican and revolutionary. Cavour and Victor Emmanuel must have had some doubt about whether even Garibaldi could maintain control over such a large army of irregular soldiers and enforce on them obedience to the cause of ' Italy and Victor Emmanuel'. It was all becoming very difficult for Cavour.

Most importantly he had to stop Garibaldi from attacking Rome. The only way to do this was to send an army from Piedmont through the Papal States to meet him before he could reach the city of Rome. Using the excuse that the Pope was unable to deal with a threatened revolt in his territory, the Piedmontese army with Victor Emmanuel at its head marched through the Papal States. They defeated a Papal army on the way, and any civilians resisting the invasion were shot as traitors to the cause of a united Italy.

In October the Piedmontese army reached Neapolitan territory and Garibaldi and Victor Emmanuel met in what should have been a highly dramatic scene, but turned out to be nothing of the sort. With a flourish of his broad-brimmed hat Garibaldi saluted Victor Emmanuel as 'the first King of Italy'. Victor Emmanuel's reply was a complete anti-climax: 'How are you, dear Garibaldi?'

In the ballots held in Sicily, Naples, Umbria and the Papal Marches there was not suprisingly an overwhelming wish for annexation by Piedmont – there seemed to be no acceptable alternative and nationalists were in the majority anyway after all the excitements of the summer.

On 7 November Victor Emmanuel and Garibaldi rode together in a triumphal state entry into Naples. One of the staff from the French embassy in Piedmont wrote an account of the events:

1   The immense popularity which Victor Emmanuel enjoys in the old provinces of Piedmont owes more to the royalist feelings of the people than to the personal qualities of the King. Events and above all the genius of his Prime Minister (Cavour) have raised him to the position
5   he now occupies in Italy and in Europe. If ever his name becomes famous in history, his only glory will have been 'to have allowed Italy to create herself.' Like all mediocre men Victor Emmanuel is jealous and quick to take offence. He will find it difficult to forget the manner of his triumphal entry into Naples, when, seated in Garibaldi's carriage –
10 Garibaldi in a red shirt – he was presented to his people by the most powerful of his subjects.
    People are mistaken in crediting Victor Emmanuel with a liking for Garibaldi. As soldiers they probably have points of contact in their characters and tastes, which have allowed them to understand each other
15 at times, but the hero's familiarity is very displeasing to the King. After all, what sovereign placed in the same situation would not resent the fabulous prestige of Garibaldi's name?

The day after the state entry into Naples Garibaldi officially handed over all his conquests to Victor Emmanuel, who in return offered him the rank of Major General, the title of Prince, a large pension and even a castle. Garibaldi refused them all because he felt that the King had behaved badly towards the Red Shirts. He had refused to inspect them and had not signed the proclamation of thanks sent to them. Soon afterwards the Garibaldini were disbanded, their services no longer required. As Garibaldi said, 'They think men are like oranges; you squeeze out the last drop of juice and then you throw away the peel'.

Garibaldi retired to his island of Caprera with a year's supply of macaroni and very little else. Both Victor Emmanuel and Cavour were determined that Garibaldi should leave active political life; as far as they were concerned his job was done. All Italy except Rome and Venetia had been united under Victor Emmanuel and the constitution of Piedmont had been extended to the whole of the new Kingdom of Italy.

Garibaldi however did not agree that his work was finished. He had his eye fixed firmly on Rome as a future target.

5 Garibaldi and Rome

Rome was still occupied by French troops protecting the Pope and there was continued pressure from Italian moderates for it to be freed and included in the new Kingdom of Italy as the historical capital.

Garibaldi had always maintained that whenever the government for political reasons found itself unable to act in the interests of national unity, it was the right of volunteers to take independent action.

Thus, in 1862 he returned to Sicily from Caprera and collected together about 3000 volunteers for the conquest of Rome. Apparently with the approval of Victor Emmanuel but not of the Piedmontese government, Garibaldi set off on the march north. He did not know that Cavour's successor as Prime Minister had planned a similar coup to that of 1860. The plan was for an invasion of Papal territory by a Piedmontese army which would reach the city of Rome before Garibaldi could. The plan needed French agreement to a Piedmontese invasion, and the plot failed because the French would not agree.

Garibaldi had already reached Palermo and been greeted with joyous shouts of 'Rome or Death'. Victor Emmanuel, sensing danger, immediately withdrew his support for Garibaldi. No one tried to stop him crossing the Straits for the message sent to the naval commander at Messina was so vague that he ignored it and allowed Garibaldi and his men to cross to Calabria. There, in bad weather, they were shot at by local troops and forced to retreat into the mountains. All except 500 of the men deserted. Those who remained were defeated at

Aspromonte in a short battle with government troops. Garibaldi, much to his annoyance, was shot in the leg and captured. He was imprisoned for a time and then returned to Caprera.

The whole adventure had turned into a disaster for Garibaldi personally and militarily. He was not used to being wounded nor to being defeated and the government too was embarrassed that the old hero, one of those responsible for the unification of Italy, had been defeated and imprisoned by the government of the kingdom which he had done so much to create.

All was not quite over for Garibaldi yet though. In 1864 the Italian government agreed to protect Rome from attack and to remove the Italian capital from Turin in Piedmont to Florence in Tuscany, an indication that they no longer wanted Rome as the capital. In return the French withdrew from Rome and in 1867 Garibaldi raised yet another army 'to capture Rome and abolish the Pope'. He and his men marched towards Rome, but he was arrested on government orders, despite the fact that he had apparently been given government support for the expedition. Without Garibaldi at their head his men continued to advance on Rome, suffering a number of defeats by Papal armies on the way. Garibaldi, meanwhile, had escaped from house arrest on Caprera and, disguised as a fisherman, had sailed in a dinghy across to the mainland where he retook command of his men. Unfortunately the planned revolution among the people of Rome failed to materialise on the date arranged, but Garibaldi was successful in defeating a Papal army.

Victor Emmanuel immediately disowned the whole affair and the French government sent an army equipped with the new breech-loading rifles back to Rome. These weapons were decisive and the Garibaldini were totally defeated. It marked the end of Garibaldi's part in Italian history, but not the end of his active life.

In 1870 after the defeat of Napoleon III by the Prussian army and the end of the Second French Empire, Garibaldi offered his services to the new French Republic. The French government hesitated to accept. After all, Garibaldi was now 63 years old, crippled with arthritis and still troubled by the wound received at Aspromonte. He did not seem the ideal choice for a military leader on active service, but, under pressure from public opinion, the French government appointed him General of the Vosges army – a hotchpotch of sharpshooters and other irregular troops, who managed under Garibaldi's leadership to defeat the Prussians in three small battles.

Afterwards he was elected to the French National Assembly in recognition of his services, but finding his fellow members unfriendly towards him, he returned to his home on the island of Caprera where he remained until his death in 1882.

Meanwhile, the French troops having been withdrawn to meet dangers from Prussia at home, Rome had been attacked and captured in 1870 by Italian troops. Garibaldi was distressed that the government should have taken what he thought was unfair advantage of Napoleon III's misfortunes. He felt it was wrong.

6 Garibaldi – An Assessment

Garibaldi's contribution to the cause of Italian unity was considerable. His flamboyant personality, his striking appearance, his theatricality, his bravery, his legendary adventures both inside and outside Italy, his success with women, all made him the centre of attention. He represented the non-intellectual active approach to Italian unity, a very different approach to that of Cavour.

As a military leader Garibaldi was a good, sometimes brilliant, commander, excellent at sizing up the situation, decisive and determined. As a guerrilla fighter he was unrivalled. He and his men were best at hand-to-hand fighting, surprise night attacks and ambushes by day. He could appear authoritarian but relied more on his strong personality rather than strict discipline to keep control over his men. Regular Italian officers who visited his camp on the outskirts of Rome in 1849 were shocked by the informality. One of them wrote:

1   Garibaldi and his officers were dressed in scarlet blouses with hats of
    every possible kind, without distinguishing marks and without any mili-
    tary insignia. They rode on (South) American saddles, and seemed to
    pride themselves on contempt for all the usual military requirements
    ... they might be seen hurrying to and fro, now dispersing, then again
5   collecting, active, rapid, untiring... We were surprised to see officers
    including the General himself leap down from their horses and attend
    to the wants of their own steeds... If they failed to obtain provisions
    from neighbouring villages, three or four colonels and majors threw
    themselves on the back of their horses and armed with long lassoes set
10 off in search of sheep or oxen.
       Garibaldi meanwhile, if the encampment was far from the scene of
    danger, would lie stretched out under his tent made from his unrolled
    saddle. If the enemy were at hand he remained constantly on horse-
    back, giving orders and visiting outposts; often, disguised as a peasant,
15 he risked his own safety in daring reconnaissances ... when the
    General's trumpet gave the signal to prepare for departure the lassoes
    served to catch the horses which had been left to graze at liberty in the
    meadows ... Garibaldi appeared more like the chief of a tribe of Indians
    than a General, but at the approach of danger, and in the heat of
20 combat, his presence of mind and courage were admirable.

Garibaldi inspired great enthusiasm and devotion in his men, firing them with the same passionate belief in Italian unity that he had himself – at least while fighting was available. During times of inaction, or if things became bad, they showed a regrettable tendency to desert.

Garibaldi's relaxed style of leadership and the general lack of discipline probably made this inevitable.

Mobility is essential in guerrilla warfare and the Garibaldini wore a lightweight uniform of the famous Red Shirt, loose trousers, boots, a cape and a broad-brimmed hat. They carried a black haversack and were armed with muskets or old rifles, sometimes with lances. In their belts they all had a heavy dagger. They needed to travel light for Garibaldi's strategy included a good deal of marching backwards and forwards to confuse the enemy and a great deal of running about with bayonets.

An important factor in Garibaldi's military success was the incompetence and lack of enthusiasm shown by the enemy. In Naples in 1860 the King and his troops were so frightened by what Garibaldi had achieved in Sicily that they put up little resistance. In Sicily he had been helped by the general confusion on the island following the peasants' revolt and by local hatred of the remaining Neapolitan troops who had an unenviable reputation for cruelty.

Nevertheless his conquest of the south was a remarkable achievement and a major element in the successful unification of Italy. He and his men accomplished it almost unaided in a very short time against all odds and expectations. Whether it was wise to unite north and south in this sudden and violent way is another matter. There was support in the south for an end to the rule by an oppressive and absolute monarch (the King of Naples), but this did not mean that there was a demand for union with Piedmont. Garibaldi and his men nearly all came from the north and had little understanding of the problems of the hot dry south. Much more could have been done for the peasants, particularly in Sicily where they were merely abandoned to the landowners. Opportunities to win popular support were missed everywhere. Perhaps if relations between Garibaldi and Cavour had been better the unsuitable Piedmontese legal and other systems would not have been introduced into southern Italy so quickly.

Garibaldi was driven by his devotion to the idea of Italian unity. Everything he did was directed at achieving it. It became an obsession and as a result he could appear to lack principles. From being a republican he had suddenly became a royalist in the service first of Charles Albert and then of Victor Emmanuel; from a supporter of popular revolution he became a supporter of the establishment. In each case he was acting in what he considered to be the best interests of Italian unity. He could have made himself a dictator of an independent southern Italy but national unity was more important to him than personal power.

He did of course have his limitations. He was not very well educated and not much of a thinker. His greatest weakness was probably his impatience for immediate action. He acted first and thought afterwards, if at all, for his actions were dominated by his heart not his head. His understanding of politics was limited. He was not interested and was often unaware of the effect his actions might have on international relations, as in his plans to march on Rome in 1860, 1862 and 1867. Even if he had been aware, it is doubtful whether he would have been at all concerned.

That chance meeting with Mazzini in 1833 had given him his ideals and his purpose in life. Although he fell out with Mazzini, he never forgot 'Young Italy' and the words '... without unity there is no true nation, without unity there is no real strength and Italy surrounded as she is by powerful, united and jealous nations, has need of strength above all things ...'.

In Garibaldi she found that strength.

References

Vyvyen Brendon, *The Making of Modern Italy* (Hodder & Stoughton, 1998)
George Trevelyan, *Garibaldi and the Making of Italy* (Longman, 1911)

Working on Chapter 4

Essentially, Chapter 4 deals with the career and achievements of just one character, the complex and controversial Giuseppe Garibaldi. What conclusions have you reached? Was he a brave adventurer and a natural leader of men who led a remarkably colourful life, or was he more – the only true patriot of the *Risorgimento* who devoted his life to the cause of Italian nationhood? The balanced conclusion reached by most historians was that he was a mixture of both. Do you agree? To really understand Garibaldi it is necessary to disregard his eccentricities and fitful lifestyle and instead concentrate on his motives and achievements. What exactly were they? To answer this objectively it is necessary to read the chapter again and make notes that identify what he saw as his mission and list his accomplishments. Outstanding was his mission with 'The Thousand' to liberate Sicily in 1860 and the daring with which he crossed to the mainland and overran southern Italy. What of his failures? In 1849, he failed in his defence of the Roman Republic and in 1862 and 1867 was involved in two unsuccessful attempts to secure the city. Other issues that need to be considered are the reasons for his change of heart that took him from being a staunch republican to a monarchist and supporter of the House of Savoy and his uneasy relationship with Count Cavour. Were the reasons for his differences with Cavour no more than a conflict between an impatient guerrilla leader and a subtle politician out to achieve his aims through diplomacy? Finally, what part did Victor Emmanuel II play in all this?

Summary Diagram

1807   Birth of Garibaldi in Nice

1820–30 Young adventurer in S. America
         Formed Red Shirts – Legionaries

1831   Chance encounter in Marseilles with Mazzini
         Converted Garibaldi to republican

1848   Returned to Italy – offered services to Charles
         Albert. Was refused but nevertheless became a
         royalist

1849   Military leader of the Roman Republic

1860   Garibaldi and 'The Thousand' – Conquest of
         the South made unification possible

1862   First of Garibaldi's efforts to take Rome failed
         and he was wounded at Aspromonte

1882   Death of Garibaldi

Answering source-based questions on Chapter 4

1. Carefully read the extract on page 71 in which a member of the
    staff of the French embassy describes the entry of Victor
    Emmanuel and Garibaldi into Naples in 1860 and the extract on
    page 74 in which an Italian officer describes the appearance of
    Garibaldi's men.

    a) (i) In the first extract what does the French diplomat mean when he
    says 'his only glory will have been 'to have allowed Italy to create her-
    self' (page 71 line 6)? (2 marks)
    (ii) In the second extract what does the Italian soldier mean when he
    refers to Garibaldi's officers as being 'without distinguishing marks and
    without any military insignia' (page 74 line 2)? (2 marks)
    b) Read the first extract again. What information can be inferred about
    the character of Victor Emmanuel II? (6 marks)
    c) How useful are the extracts to an understanding of the character of

Garibaldi? In your answer use relevant background knowledge as well as information derived from the extracts. (*10 marks*)

Answering essay questions on Chapter 4

1. 'Without doubt, he was the greatest of the Italian patriots and without his efforts, unification would have taken much longer to achieve.' How valid is this estimate of Garibaldi's importance to Italian unification? (*25 marks*)
2. How important was the contribution of Garibaldi to the cause of Italian unification? Explain your answer fully. (*25 marks*)

These questions are typical of those asked about Garibaldi. The first question is based on a quotation whilst the second is more straightforward and traditional in approach. Although they represent different styles in questioning, the answers required will, to some extent, follow a similar pattern. Both questions require a critical survey of Garibaldi's achievements but more is needed that a simple, accurate and fact-filled narrative. In question 1, it is necessary to consider firstly if Garibaldi was 'the greatest of Italian patriots'. Only by comparing his achievements with those of Mazzini, Cavour and Victor Emmanuel can we do this. In reaching your conclusion, remember to produce an argument with supportive reasons. The second part of the question is easier since few would dispute that unification would have taken longer had it not been for Garibaldi's liberation of Sicily and Naples. What of his failed attempts to take Rome and his feuding with Cavour? Might these have been impediments to unification? Whilst question 2 requires a detailed account of Garibaldi's contribution to Italian unification, the central issue of the question is 'how important' his contribution was. Avoid leaving your assessment to the final paragraph and try to show some on-going appreciation of Garibaldi's importance throughout your answer.

Working on multi-source questions on Chapter 4

Source A

1 'If Garibaldi means to go, he is sufficiently strong and supported by public opinion to be able to go whether the government likes it or not.'

[*A view expressed by the British representative in Piedmont in 1860.*]

Source B

1 'In Sicily, Garibaldi has let himself become intoxicated with his success. Instead of carrying annexation, or allowing it to be carried, he dreams of conquering Naples and delivering Italy. If moderating councils came

to him from England, for which he has great respect, that would be
5 most advantageous.'

[A view expressed by Count Cavour in 1860.]

Source C

1 'Conqueror of the Kingdom of the Sicilies, Garibaldi had won himself an
extraordinary position and flatterers around him had every interest in
increasing it still further. His boundless pride had been over-excited by
the praises... Arrogant towards the government, insolent to parlia-
5 ment, he spared the deputies no insults. Many Italians found it hard to
believe that their hero was no more than a poor simpleton, brave no
doubt but with pride that destroyed his common sense.'

[An entry in the diary of a French diplomat in 1860.]

Source D

1 'Garibaldi was at his wits end to divert attention from himself to the
King ... keeping his horse a few paces behind he cried, 'This is Vittorio
Emmanuele, your King, the King of Italy.' The peasants stared and lis-
tened and then not understanding again shouted, "Viva Gairibardo!".'

[An account given by a supporter of Garibaldi of his leader's meeting with the King in
Naples in 1861.]

Source E

1 'Garibaldi commanded his men in person and endeavoured many times
to check the retreat of his men. They could not, however, stand against
the greater coolness and steadiness of the advance of the regular
troops.'

5
  [An account given by an American diplomat of Garibaldi's behaviour at the Battle of
Mentana in 1867.]

Source F

1 'Garibaldi showed the type of courage ... that befits a bandit leader
from the woods... We in Italy know that puppets are made of painted
rags and sticks. The puppeteer can dress them as king or clown alternatively, he can bring them on to the stage as he wishes and then hang
5 them up in a locker until the time comes to pack up and move to a new
place.'

[Garibaldi as described by a Catholic priest in 1869.]

a) (i) In what ways do Sources C and F agree in their assessment of
        Garibaldi? (5 marks)

  (ii) Comment on the reliability of Sources D and F. (5 marks)

b) (i) Compare Sources A, B and D. To what extent do Sources B and
        D support the impression given in Source A regarding the extent
        of the popularity of Garibaldi? (5 marks)

(ii) To what extent does Source F contradict the views expressed in Sources A and E?

c) How full an understanding do the sources provide of the character of Garibaldi? In your answer use your own relevant knowledge as well as information derived from the sources. (*10 marks*)

Napoleon III and Italy

This is quite a short chapter which should not give you any difficulty in a first reading. It is important though to make sure you understand the part played by Napoleon III in the unification of Italy, and why he acted as he did. Why was Napoleon III of France interested in what was happening in Italy? What were his aims there and was he successful in achieving them?

KEY DATES

1849 Napoleon III to rescue of the Pope – Roman Republic attacked by French troops who remained in Rome until 1870.

1858 Orsini plot to assassinate Napoleon III – leads Napoleon to decide to 'do something for Italy'.

1858 Meeting at Plombières with Cavour – plot to involve Austria in war and free Lombardy and Venetia from foreign rule.

1859 Battles of Magenta and Solferino. War with Austria ended by Armistice of Villafranca. Lombardy returned to Italy via Napoleon who had already gone back home to France.

1866 Treaty of Prague. Germany surrendered Venetia to Italy.

1870 French troops withdrawn from Rome to fight in the Franco-Prussian war.

1873 Napoleon III died in exile in Britain.

1 Napoleon III Emperor of France

The family of Napoleon Bonaparte, Napoleon I, was exiled from France by the Vienna Settlement of 1815. Some of the members of the family were in Italy during the winter of 1830–1. Among them was Louis Napoleon Bonaparte, Napoleon I's nephew, who became involved in a wild and foolish scheme to capture the Pope's castle of Saint Angelo. He led a conspiracy which planned to proclaim his cousin, the son of Napoleon I, as King of Italy. As his cousin was a prisoner of the Austrians, Louis Napoleon would rule as regent on his behalf. The secret was not well kept and the authorities had little difficulty in discovering the plot and arresting those involved. Louis Napoleon was expelled from Rome and went to join the rest of his family in Florence where he almost immediately became entangled in another conspiracy involving Modena and the Papal States.

At this time Napoleon was still a young man, only 22, inexperienced and full of romantic, impracticable dreams and schemes, but with genuine if vague liberal ideas. The conspiracies of 1830–1 mark the beginning of his love affair with Italian nationalism, and although his actions were often unpredictable, his wish to help the Italians was sincere. In the end it was to be with his aid that Italian independence and unity was achieved, although in 1849 no one could have foreseen it.

In March 1849 the Roman Republic was proclaimed with Mazzini at its head and Garibaldi as its military leader. The Pope, who had taken refuge in Naples, appealed to the Catholic monarchs of Europe, but no help came. Only Louis Napoleon, recently elected as President of the French Republic, was prepared to act. The Austrians who were already occupying Tuscany and the northern part of the Papal States would soon be threatening Rome itself. Napoleon knew there was no time to lose if he was to benefit from the situation by restoring the Pope and winning the approval of the Church which would go with it.

The French Assembly agreed to Napoleon's plan of providing an expeditionary force to be sent to Rome, and 10,000 troops set sail in April. Their commander was well received when they landed in the Papal states near Rome and confidently expected a similar welcome from the citizens of Rome itself. He was not all prepared for the strong resistance organised by Mazzini and Garibaldi. A Bonaparte could not begin his Presidency of France with a military defeat, and so Louis Napoleon, when the news reached him, agreed to a temporary armistice which would give him time to reinforce his army. This done, the now over 20,000 strong French army attacked the outskirts of Rome at the beginning of June, and a month later the city fell. It was quickly restored to a reactionary government of the Papal governing body, the Papal Curia, while the French stood by. Whatever Louis Napoleon had intended, he had achieved nothing by his expedition except loss of life. The government of Rome was again as it had been – backward and oppressive.

In December 1852 Napoleon assumed the title of Emperor Napoleon III. He declared that France wanted peace, but quickly found himself fighting against Russia in defence of Turkey in the Crimean War which broke out in 1854. Among France's allies was Piedmont, and when the war ended in 1856, Cavour too had a seat at the peace conference in Paris. This brought the two men into close contact, with important long-term consequences for them both. After the conference ended, they kept in touch through mutual friends and through Napoleon's nephew, Cavour's private secretary, and the young and beautiful Countess Castiglione.

On a number of occasions in the 1850s Napoleon spoke to Cavour about 'doing something for Italy' but did not explain what that something should be. It is difficult now to know what, if anything, he had in mind. It is usually taken to mean that he wished as part of his anti-Austrian policy to drive Austria out of northern Italy, leaving the way

Napoleon III on horseback.

clear for Piedmont and consequently for France to influence events in northern Italy. It may have been that as a romantic but sincere supporter of Italian independence Napoleon wished to be helpful to the cause. After all, in 1830 he had been a Carbonaro or something of the kind. He may also have been influenced by family tradition – Napoleon I had taken over Italy at the beginning of the nineteenth century. He would only be continuing the Napoleonic legend. Although he had none of the qualities, the determination and the gifts of leadership which Napoleon I had possessed, he saw himself as a leader of 'the peoples of Europe' in their search for freedom and national identity.

What did Napoleon mean when he talked about 'Italy'? Some historians believe that before 1861 'Italy' to him meant northern Italy, the old Napoleonic Kingdom of Italy, made up of states like Piedmont, already substantially French in character as a reflection of the occupying forces at the beginning of the century, and where French was still the language of the educated minority. At this stage it is doubtful whether Napoleon would have wanted the whole Italian peninsula united into a single kingdom. Such a united country might become a threat to France itself.

Napoleon's plans were always fluid, complex and unclear, capable of being changed at any moment, and because they were also extremely secret, very difficult to unravel. It seems probable that, as far as Italy was concerned, they were based on driving out the Austrians and the setting up of a French-controlled, enlarged Piedmont. This new Piedmont would be large enough to be a useful ally for France, but not so large as to be able to do without France, to oppose French wishes or to be a threat to France itself. It must certainly not be allowed to become strong enough to interfere with French ambitions to acquire Nice and Savoy.

Central Italy could be part of the new Piedmont or could be a separate French-controlled state, perhaps governed by one of Napoleon's many cousins. Other cousins could rule Naples and Sicily. The Pope would be persuaded to agree to all these arrangements by being made President of an Italian Federation of States. It seemed to Napoleon a splendid plan which would please everyone: Italian nationalists because the Austrians had been driven out; moderate nationalists by the end of the old absolute governments; Victor Emmanuel and Cavour by the expansion of Piedmont; the clergy by an increase in the political power of the Pope; French nationalists by the acquisition of new territory and the replacement of Austrian influence in Italy by that of France; and last, but not least, the Bonaparte family by an extension of family power and prestige.

Napoleon moved into action in January 1858 when an attempt was made on his life. A group of four Italians, led by Count Felice Orsini was responsible. Orsini had been a refugee in London, where he had had three large bombs specially made for him. The four men took the bombs from London to Paris via Brussels, by train, completely outwitting the French police who had been tipped off that they would be arriving by road. The bombs were thrown at Napoleon and the Empress Eugenie as their coach arrived at the opera. Eight people died and about 150 were injured.

Orsini seems to have believed that if he killed Napoleon a new republican government in France would come to the assistance of Italy. At his trial, a letter, said to have been written by Orsini in his prison cell, was read out. In it Orsini appealed to Napoleon to help Italy achieve independence and by doing so to receive the blessings of 25 million Italian citizens. There is some evidence that Napoleon himself encouraged Orsini to write this letter and may even have dictated its contents. He certainly arranged for it to be published. It is still not known whether the letter was a genuine plea from an Italian patriot or whether it was organised by Napoleon to provide him with an excuse to intervene in Italy.

Napoleon wasted no time. He began by meeting Cavour at Plombières on 21 July 1858 where they hatched the plot to lure Austria into war. Napoleon agreed that if it were done in a non-revolutionary way, he would support Piedmont in an attempt to recover Lombardy and Venetia. The difficulty was that Piedmont could only provide 100,000 of the 300,000 troops needed. French military assistance might in the end be required, as indeed it was, in the War of 1859 (details of the war and what happened afterwards are on pages 50–53).

2 Napoleon and the Unification of Italy

> **KEY ISSUE** What was Napoleon's attitude to Garibaldi's successes in southern Italy?

After Garibaldi's successful conquest of Sicily in July 1860 the European powers woke up to the fact that he clearly intended to attack the Neapolitan mainland. Should he be allowed to do so, was the question being asked in diplomatic circles everywhere. In a flurry of activity only Britain among the Great Powers had any sympathy with Garibaldi's aims. Napoleon found himself in difficulties. He did not want to offend Britain by trying to stop Garibaldi, but he did not want to see Garibaldi take over Naples and threaten Rome and the Pope. He suggested to Britain a naval blockade of the Straits of Messina to make it impossible for Garibaldi to leave Sicily for the mainland. Britain refused and Garibaldi crossed the Straits successfully in the middle of August, meeting only token resistance from the Neapolitan navy which had already agreed with Garibaldi not to interfere with the crossing.

When Cavour's army entered the Papal States on 11 September to prevent Garibaldi and his army from reaching Rome, Napoleon had to disapprove in public of what was no less than unprovoked invasion of a neighbouring state. There is evidence to suggest that he had made a secret agreement with Cavour that France would not interfere as long as Garibaldi did not reach Rome. French diplomatic relations with Piedmont were broken off, but this seems to have been only a temporary move, no more than a gesture by Napoleon and not to be taken seriously.

3 Venetia and Rome

> **KEY ISSUES** Italian unification was not yet complete. Rome and Venetia were still to be freed from foreign occupation. How was this done and how far was the final success due to Napoleon?

a) Venetia

In 1866 the question of Venetia came to a head. In a secret treaty with Prussia, which was already engaged in a struggle with Austria for control of Germany, it was agreed that if Prussia went to war with Austria within two months, Italy would follow Prussia and declare war on Austria. Napoleon agreed with Prussia to remain neutral and at the end of the war to receive Venetia if Austria were defeated. Italy would in turn receive Venetia from Napoleon as a reward for providing a second front in the Austro-Prussian war.

Knowing now that Italy would receive Venetia if Prussia won, Napoleon needed to make sure that the same thing would happen if Austria won. He therefore signed a secret treaty with Austria in which it was agreed that if Austria defeated Prussia, Venetia would be ceded, that is officially handed over to France, and passed on by Napoleon to Italy. In return France would remain neutral during the war. These complicated arrangements are a good example of the double-dealing for which Napoleon was famous throughout Europe and which gave him a bad reputation. Whatever happened he made sure he would always win.

The war, known in Germany as the Seven Weeks' War and in Italy as the Third War of Independence, began on 24 June 1866. Italy was defeated by Austria ten days later, mainly because of poor Italian military leadership. On 3 July Austria was in turn defeated by Prussia at Koniggratz, also known as Sadova, which was yet another horrific battle. Around the Prussian soldiers 'bombshells crashed through clay walls as if they were cardboard; the village in which they were sheltering was set on fire. Chunks of wood and big tree splinters flew around our heads. We felt we were in God's hands'. Austrian soldiers too suffered when 4000 men set out to attack the Prussian guns, a venture from which only

1800 badly wounded men returned. About 60,000 Austrian soldiers tried to reach the safety of Koniggratz, only to be drowned in water released from the waterworks which protected the town. As before there was inadequate provision for looking after the wounded left lying for up to three days on the 45 square miles of the battlefield. The Prussians lost almost 2000 men, the Austrians nearer 6000. The war came to an end with the Peace of Prague in August 1866. By it, Austria immediately gave up Venetia to Napoleon who in turn surrendered it, as agreed, to Italy. Welcome as the return of Venetia was, there was a feeling of humiliation in Italy about the way in which it had been done, not by Italians, but only as the result of action by the Great Powers of Austria, Prussia and France. Italians tried to console themselves with the idea that there was now only the need to recover Rome and deal with the Pope for unification to be complete.

b) Rome

The outstanding problem was how to get rid of the French garrison in Rome. Until then the work of driving out the foreigners would not have been completed. How could it be done?

In July1870 the Franco-Prussian War broke out. In an unexpected piece of good fortune for Italy, very soon after the war began Napoleon needed reinforcements to bring his army up to strength and withdrew his troops from Rome. The Italian government made no immediate move to take over the city, but on 1 September 1870 with Napoleon heavily defeated and taken prisoner by the Prussians, they felt it safe to take action. Victor Emmanuel, whose daughter was married to Napoleon's cousin, felt he ought to send an army to rescue Napoleon, but his government thought otherwise. Italy had been neutral in the war and must remain so. This did not mean, though, that they could not take advantage of Napoleon's misfortunes to settle the question of Rome once and for all.

On 8 September Victor Emmanuel sent a letter to the Pope suggesting an agreement. The Pope would have to give up his Temporal Power, which since 1849 had depended on the support of the French troops in Rome. As these were no longer available, Victor Emmanuel urged the Pope to allow Rome to become at last the capital of a united Italy and to settle for an arrangement of the kind suggested by Cavour ten years earlier. This would separate Church and State and, although removing from the Pope his Temporal Power (his right to rule over the Papal States as a Prince), it would allow him to keep his Spiritual Power as Head of the Church and this would be safeguarded and guaranteed by the Italian State.

Victor Emmanuel added :

I, being a Catholic King and an Italian and, as such, guardian ... by the national will of ... all the Italians, feel it my duty to take, in the face of Europe and Catholicity, the responsibility of maintaining order in the

peninsula and the safety of the Holy See... The Head of Catholicity sur-
5 rounded by the devotion of the Italian people, should preserve on the
banks of the Tiber a glorious seat independent of every human sover-
eignty. Your Holiness by liberating Rome from foreign troops will take
from her the constant danger of being the battleground of outside
forces.

Three days later the Pope replied sharply and to the point:

I cannot admit the demands of your letter, nor accept the principles
contained in it.

As a result of this unhelpful reply the government felt they had no
choice but to act. They decided to send an army of 6,000 troops to
occupy Rome. Papal troops fought back briefly but the city was
shelled by government artillery and a breach made in the walls. On 20
September 1870 Victor Emmanuel's army entered Rome. In October
Romans voted overwhelmingly for union with the rest of Italy and
Rome became the capital city of a politically and geographically
united Italy. The new Kingdom of Italy seemed to be complete. That
it was still severely flawed socially and economically was not mentioned, least of all by Victor Emmanuel of Piedmont, now King Victor
Emmanuel II of Italy, or by his government of moderate liberal politicians. At the first session of the first Parliament to be held in the new
capital, disregarding the still unsolved problem of what to do about
the Pope, the King declared: 'The work to which we consecrated our
lives is accomplished'.

As worldly power began to slip from his grasp, the Pope concen-
trated on strengthening his spiritual power over the Church and its
members. In 1864 Pius IX, who had once been thought of as being so
progressive, had published the controversial *Syllabus of Errors,* which,
turning the Church away from the real world, condemned among
other things liberal politics and religious toleration. In July 1870 he
went further with the Doctrine of Papal Infallibility, which decreed
that the Pope's spiritual judgement could not be challenged at the
time or afterwards for he was the supreme judge of truth for the
Catholic Church. Three months later when Rome became the capital
city of Italy the Pope found himself left with only 109 acres of land
making up the area called the Patrimony of Saint Peter. He retired
into his palace of the Vatican where he described himself as its 'prisoner'. He was offered a state pension but refused it, and instead
excommunicated Victor Emmanuel and the government. Without
Napoleon III's troops he could do nothing to change his situation or
prevent the separation of Church and State in the new Kingdom of
Italy.

References

James Macmillan, *Napoleon III* (Longman, 1991)

Summary Diagram

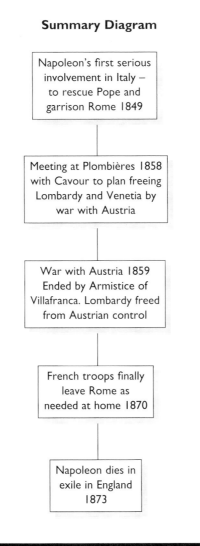

Napoleon's first serious
involvement in Italy –
to rescue Pope and
garrison Rome 1849

Meeting at Plombières 1858
with Cavour to plan freeing
Lombardy and Venetia by
war with Austria

War with Austria 1859
Ended by Armistice of
Villafranca. Lombardy freed
from Austrian control

French troops finally
leave Rome as
needed at home 1870

Napoleon dies in
exile in England
1873

Working on Chapter 5

Chapter 5 is concerned with the part played by France and, more
especially Napoleon III, in the events leading to the unification of
Italy. Two issues emerge. Firstly, to what extent did the French
emperor work in the interests of his own country rather than those of
Italy? Remember, Napoleon III was a notorious conspirator and
wheeler-dealer and was always prepared to be part of behind-the-
scenes scheming. He used cunning and duplicity not only in his
dealings with Cavour and Victor Emmanuel II, but also in his
relations with the leaders of other European powers. Secondly, would

the unification of Italy have been achieved without the involvement of the other great European powers, particularly France?

Structured questions based on Chapter 5

1. **a)** Explain the significance of the Orsini Plot of 1858. (*4 marks*)
   b) To what extent might Napoleon III's attitude to Italian independence be considered erratic and unpredictable? (*6 marks*)
   c) Would it be justifiable to claim that Napoleon III's involvement in Italian affairs was only undertaken when it was to the advantage of France? (*10 marks*)

2. **a)** **(i)** What did Victor Emmanuel II mean by 'responsibility for maintaining order in the peninsula and the safety of the Holy See' (pages 87–88 lines 1–4)? (*2 marks*)
   (ii) What is meant by 'the Pope's spiritual judgement could not be challenged' (page 88)? (*2 marks*)
   b) **(i)** Why was it necessary for French troops to be garrisoned in Rome? (*3 marks*)
   (ii) What circumstances made it possible for Italian troops to occupy Rome in 1870? (*3 marks*)
   c) Distinguish between the Pope's 'temporal' and 'spiritual' powers. (*5 marks*)
   d) With what justification could the Pope refer to himself as a 'prisoner' after 1870? (*5 marks*)

The Kingdom of Italy 1860–70

POINTS TO CONSIDER

After 1861, what was the newly proclamed Kingdom of Italy like? Did it improve life for Italians? Who do you think united Italy? As there are a number of possible candidates, make sure you are able to make a good case for your choice(s).

KEY DATES

1860   March Tuscany, Parma and Modena united with Piedmont
   Nice and Savoy handed over to France in return for France
   agreeing to the enlargement of Piedmont.
   April   Garibaldi's expedition of 'The Thousand' to Sicily.
   May   Conquest of Sicily by Garibaldi.
   July   Conquest of Naples by Garibaldi completed.
   September   Piedmont's invasion of the Papal States. Garibaldi
                    handed over all southern Italy to Victor Emmanuel.
   October   Southern Italy voted for union with Piedmont.
1861 **March**   The Kingdom of Italy proclaimed with Turin as its
                    capital. Victor Emmanuel II of Piedmont became
                    Victor Emmanuel II of Italy.
1862   Garibaldi's march on Rome halted at Aspromonte and Garibaldi
   wounded.
1864   Capital moved from Turin to Florence. Pope published 'Syllabus of
   Errors' condemning everything modern.
1866   Venetia added to the Kingdom of Italy.
1867   Garibaldi's final attempt to march on Rome failed.
1870   French troops left Rome and were replaced by Italian troops.
   Rome named as capital of the Kingdom of Italy. The Pope refused
   to recognise the new state and retreated into the Vatican. In July
   published the doctrine of Papal Infallibility.

1 The Kingdom of Italy

> **KEY ISSUES** What was the new Kingdom of Italy like during the
> first decade of its existence? Did it make any difference to the
> lives of its inhabitants? Was Italy truly united by 1870?

After the proclamation of Victor Emmanuel II as King of Italy in 1861,
Piedmont's Prime Minister D'Azeglio remarked 'Italy is made, now we
must make Italians'. Victor Emmanuel II, scornful of his new subjects,

annexed to Piedmont
April 1860

ceded to France and
passed to Italy by
Napoleon III July 1866

FRANCE

SAVOY
TO FRANCE
1860

LOMBARDY
(1860)

VENETIA
(1866)

AUSTRIA

Magenta ╳

Solferino ╳ ╳ Custozza

● Venice

● Turin

PIEDMONT

PARMA
(1860)

ROMAGNA
(1860)

OTTOMAN
EMPIRE

TO FRANCE
1860

NICE

MODENA
(1860)

LUCCA

TUSCANY
(1860)

PAPAL
STATES
(1860)

ADRIATIC SEA

KINGDOM OF SARDINIA PIEDMONT

CORSICA
(FRENCH)

new capital
of Italy 1870

● Rome
(1870)

NAPLES
(1860)

Patrimony of St. Peter
- all that was left to
Pope by 1870

● Naples

SARDINIA

KINGDOM OF THE
TWO SICILIES
(1860)

╳ Aspromonte

MEDITERRANEAN SEA

Palermo ●

SICILY

Garibaldi defeated
and wounded 1862

N

km	0		150
miles	0		100

The Kingdom of Italy 1859–70
(Dates in brackets indicate the date each state was unified with Piedmont.)

who did not seem to understand that they now belonged to the 'nation' of which he was head, voiced his opinion that 'There are only two ways of governing Italians, by bayonets and by bribery'.

a) The Road to Political Unification

Unification was not complete in 1861. Not until 1866 was Venetia successfully won back from Austria with the help of Napoleon III of France, despite a serious defeat for Italy by the Austrian navy. Garibaldi made two unsuccessful attempts in 1862 and 1867 to invade and take Rome, but it was not until 1870 that the city became part of a united Italy when Napoleon III ordered his occupying troops to withdraw because they were needed to defend France. The city of Rome was the obvious natural capital of Italy and failure to include it in 1860 had been a grave disappointment to Italian liberals. 1870 saw this disappointment turn to joy when Rome was at last declared the capital and Italian troops were welcomed as they marched in to replace the French garrison, which had been, a long unwanted foreign presence in the city.

Pope Pius IX did not join in the rejoicing because he still feared a further attack on Rome by revolutionaries. He was deeply distressed at the loss of his French protectors and worried by what he called 'the triumph of disorder and the victory of wicked revolution' as the Piedmontese army moved into and took over the major part of the Papal States. This brought to an end the Pope's Temporal (worldly, territorial) power which he had always claimed to be a necessary addition to his Spiritual (religious) power. He withdrew into the Vatican, the Papal residence, as its self-proclaimed 'prisoner', determined to demonstrate his continued spiritual importance. As head of the Catholic Church, he announced that any Catholics who took part in Italian politics or worked for the new secular state would be excommunicated. They would not be able to receive communion or in some cases even to enter a church. If they died excommunicated they would be unable to be buried by a priest or in consecrated ground.

Through its beliefs, rituals and language, the Catholic Church had always been the main unifying element within the country. Even though Catholicism remained the state religion even after the Pope retreated into the Vatican as its 'prisoner', the many liberal-minded Catholics who supported the new secular (worldly, non-religious) government, but who wished also to keep the faith, found themselves in difficulties. The old balanced relationship between Church and State no longer existed. It threatened instead to become a hostile clash of personalities and values, as over the next two decades the Pope became ever more hostile to the Italian State.

Apart from the question of the Pope, the government found itself with a number of other problems, which the poor qualities of most of Cavour's successors as Prime Minister during the 1860s did nothing to help. None was charismatic, none had the leadership qualities of the heroes of the *Risorgimento*. Many remained in power for only a short time. Farrini, who suffered a mental breakdown, tried to knife the King and was removed from office after only three months, and Ratazzi became involved in Garibaldi's failed attacks on Rome in 1862 and 1867 and was forced to resign. Some Italian historians still argue though that in their own way members of the Italian governments in the 1860s and 1870s did good work establishing the new kingdom and that they were just as successful and important as those of earlier years. In 1928 the Italian philosopher Benedetto Croce wrote a spirited defence of the government as made up of 'men of noble and self-sacrificing character' and 'upright and loyal gentlemen'. Other historians, such as the Communist Antonio Gramsci, described the government as made up of moderate liberals who had managed to outwit the democratic republicans and take over the government.

The Italy of 1861 was a constitutional monarchy, not the republic that Mazzini had dreamed about and worked for, nor a federation under the Pope as Gioberti and later Cavour and Napoleon III had proposed. The constitution was based on Charles Albert's *Statuto* of 1848, and the sovereign body was the King in Parliament and not 'the People' as Mazzini had hoped.

The new regime did not turn Italy into a true democracy, but only into what has been described as an unsatisfactory parliamentary democracy. The government was made up of members of the Piedmontese nobility and educated middle-class minority who formed an elite, and the all-male Parliament was elected by a very narrow framework of voters. These too were all male, over 25 years old, literate and tax-paying – about two per cent of the population – and most of them from northern Italy. It was not surprising that Parliament consisted almost entirely of well-to-do traditionally minded liberals and was totally unrepresentative of the mass of the people.

However, some progress was made towards a more unified nation. The various legal codes or collections of laws of individual states were formed into a single penal (criminal) code based on that of Piedmont and quickly introduced everywhere except Tuscany, which kept its own moderate code. In 1865 a single system of civil law similar to France's *Code Napoleon* was adopted throughout the country. It allowed civil marriage, although divorce remained illegal. As might have been expected, the foreign policy, foreign ministry and diplomatic service of the Kingdom were based on those of Piedmont.

During the 1860s a unified Italian army was formed out of the old armies of Piedmont, Naples and the Central Italian states, plus Garibaldi's 'Army of the South'. The whole army was modernised and reorganised along Prussian lines. Later, the navies of Piedmont and Naples were amalgamated into a single force, although not until 1876 was there any attempt at modernising or reorganising it. Schools and universities came under state control as part of a policy to provide a unified system of education throughout the peninsula.

The government was faced with serious geographical, social, political and economic problems by the need to unite two very different areas of the country – the prosperous, semi-industrialised 'advanced' north comprising of Piedmont and her immediate neighbours, with the poor, agriculturally based 'backward' south, the regions to the south of the Papal States.

b) North and South

> **KEY ISSUES** What were the main divisions between northern and southern Italy? How did the government deal with them? How far was it successful in uniting north and south by 1870?

Faced with the need to find some way of uniting north and south Cavour realised how difficult this would be. He claimed that 'To harmonize the north with the south is more difficult than to fight Austria or to struggle with Rome'.

The new government in the north at first tried to deal with the problem by ignoring it and making no attempt to understand it. When that did not work it used the quite unsuitable solution of forcing a Piedmontese style of government on the south. It was unsuitable because in Naples and Sicily, the problems were not so much political as social and economic. The majority of the population was illiterate, lived in poverty and squalor, and at a level of near starvation. As the small number of great landowners continued to enclose land to add to their estates, known as *latifundia* (Latin – lati = wider; funda = estate), there was less and less land left available for the multitude of peasants. When the old common lands disappeared into the great estates, peasant families could not feed themselves as they had done before, for they did not now have land on which to graze cattle or to grow crops. The government again showed its total lack of understanding of the situation by introducing higher taxation. The cost of living rose and the quality of peasant life fell even lower as they struggled to pay the new taxes. Their life was further complicated by new, difficult to understand, legal systems and, worst of all, by conscription which took the young men away from the farms where they were needed. In 1861 around 25,000 of them took to the hills of Naples and Sicily to avoid military service. They scraped a living as bandits instead. Many in the west of Sicily joined the Mafia which, taking advantage of the general social unrest, was thriving, as public opinion in the south turned not just against the landowners but also against Victor Emmanuel II and Piedmont. Peasant families began migrating to the towns in search of work and, often finding none, became part of the growing underclass of semi-destitute people whose only hope of food and shelter was to turn to crime. This was particularly the case in Palermo, the capital of Sicily, and in the overcrowded city of Naples where the respectable citizens were 'put in fear of their lives' by half-starved beggars.

In the early 1860s law and order, never very strong in Sicily and Naples, broke down totally. Bandits became bolder and more numerous as rural discontent fuelled a revolution which soon turned into a civil war in which more people were killed than in all the revolutions and wars of the *Risorgimento*. A Piedmontese army of some 100,000 men was called in to suppress the disorder. It took them four years, from 1861 to 1865, to do so.

Government ministers still made no real attempt to understand what was happening in the south. Naples, they believed, was 'rotten'. Neapolitans were 'barbarians', idle, politically corrupt, and backward. They brought their troubles on themselves by their laziness, sitting about in the sun instead of working. At the root of the government attitude were the beliefs in the rightness of Cavour's original plan to reorganise the whole peninsula on the Piedmontese model, and in the idea that the south held great wealth, just waiting for the north to take and use it. On both counts they were wrong, and attempts to put them into practice only had the effect of increasing the growth of industry in the north while making matters socially and economically worse in the south. Throughout the 1860s north and south remained as far apart as ever.

2 Social and Economic Changes

a) The Standard of Living

This fell throughout Italy for all social classes as the government struggled to balance the books. In the mid-1860s, when Venetia was added to the Kingdom, government spending increased until it exceeded income by 60 per cent. The level of taxation was decided not by Parliament but by the King alone, and unfortunately his main interest was in making war, the most expensive activity any country can indulge in. To pay for his military activities taxes had to rise, and in 1868 the unpopular tax on grinding corn was revived. The increased taxes fell most heavily on peasants everywhere, who could least afford to pay. Many, finding they could not survive on the produce of their few acres, moved into the towns, as large numbers of others had done before them.

b) The Place of Women

For the first time extensive research has been done on this topic in recent years by Italian historians. After unification, women found themselves at first, as they had been before, second-class citizens in a macho society – both in the home where in all social classes a wife was legally and actually subject to her husband, and in the workplace where working women were actively discouraged from joining the new mutual-aid societies which were the forerunners of trade unions. In 1862 only about 10,000 women, as opposed to about 100,000 men, were members, and women continued to be paid half as much as men for the same work and the same long hours.

In the 1860s in the towns, the availability of cheap housing close to factories, which is where most of the work was available, became very important to working women. They were no longer restricted to out-work in the home or to labouring in quarries, fields or on the roads. Until the 1870s women continued to work at home, especially once the treadle sewing machine came into use, but increasing numbers of women moved into the factories.

For many the work was making cigars, a job done exclusively by women. In one of the 20 state-owned factories, 500 workers produced 700 kilos of cigars a day. The hours were long and the pay low, but there was company in the rows of workers sitting side by side on high stools in the large warm rooms. Unfortunately, there was widespread tuberculosis, caused by the overcrowded and unsanitary housing of the poor and by the fact that workers were undernourished. There was then no treatment. It only needed one infected woman to be working in an unventilated workroom and dozens alongside her would catch it. Factory records show that hundreds of women on their books died from the disease.

In the textile trades women had always been employed spinning, knitting and sewing, although the strength needed to operate the heavy wooden looms meant that weaving was usually done by men. After 1860 outwork in the home still continued – in 1861 300,000 peasant women were spinning flax and hemp at home and this number rose to nearly a million as peasant incomes fell and women needed to earn extra money. Unfortunately almost every job women turned their hands to brought them illness and deformity, whether it was making leather gloves on a cumbersome sewing machine which meant hours of working in a cramped position; or catching a fever standing in dirty and cold stagnant water up to their waists for hours at a time steeping (soaking) flax and hemp ready for spinning; or working along with their children in the newly planted rice fields of Piedmont and Lombardy, their feet and legs in muddy water from one hour after dawn until one hour before sunset as they tended the rice plants. As a result, death from malaria was common among the rice workers.

Working in hazardous conditions in the factories seemed preferable to many women. In Piedmont alone 36,000 women worked in the silk industry in factories where their hands were ruined not by water which was hot, but by water which was kept boiling and into which they had to plunge their hands in the process of reeling the silk thread off the cocoons.

The old domestic standbys of spinning and weaving came to an end when competition from the new cotton cloth imports shook the textile industry to its foundations and led to change. From the late 1860s onwards, cloth production moved into the factory and into the machine age, a move which had an unexpected effect on family life.

Spinning and weaving in the home had previously involved the whole family – bringing together men, women and children. Factory work destroyed the family as a self-contained production unit, changed the division of labour between men and women, resulted in a great increase in the number of babies left at the foundling hospitals to free their mothers for work, and in many cases destroyed family harmony and peace. The introduction of mechanised looms in the factories eliminated the heavy work of weaving previously done by men. They found themselves no longer needed and replaced as weavers by women and girls who were cheaper to employ, often leaving the men without work. This disturbed the long-accepted social relationships within peasant and other working families because, for the first time on any large scale, male domination was challenged as women became independent wage-earners outside the home.

3 Unification

> **KEY ISSUES** What exactly was the *Risorgimento* and how important was it in the unification of Italy? Who united Italy?

a) Mazzini's View of the Kingdom of Italy

In 1871 Mazzini, who had hoped for so long for a free and united Italy, criticised it when, ten years after the Kingdom of Italy was declared, as a still suspect revolutionary republican, he was not allowed to take the seat in Parliament to which he had been elected:

1   The Italy which we represent today, like it or not, is a living lie. Not only do foreigners own Italian territory on our frontiers with France and Germany, but even if we possessed Nice and Trieste, we should still have only ... the dead corpse of Italy.

5   Italy was put together just as though it were a piece of lifeless mosaic, and the battles which made this mosaic were fought by foreign rulers who should have been loathed as our common enemies. Lombardy, scene of the great Five Days in 1848, allowed herself to be joined to Italy by a French despot. The Venetians, despite their heroic
10   defence in 1849, come to us by kind permission of a German monarch. The best of us once fought against France for possession of Rome... Southern Italy was won by volunteers and a real movement of the

people, but then it resigned its early promise and gave in to a government which still refuses to give Italy a new national constitution.
15 The battles fought by Italy in this process were defeats. Custozza was lost because of the incompetence or worse of our leaders. Italians are now without a new constitution that could express their will. We can therefore have no real national existence or international policy of our own. In domestic politics ... we are governed by a few rich men ...
20 Ordinary people are disillusioned. They had watched ... as Italy, once ruler of the civilised world, began to rise again; but now they turn away their eyes and say to themselves: 'this is just the ghost of Italy.

Why was Mazzini so critical of the new Kingdom? After all, some of his hopes had been fulfilled. He might fret about the loss of Italian-speaking Nice, but the Austrians had gone, Lombardy and Venetia were back in Italian hands and Rome had become the capital city. It was the way in which it had happened which he found so difficult to accept. Italy was free and the states were united politically but they were not united socially or economically. The division between the prosperous north and the impoverished south had not been resolved. 'Italy had not made herself' as he and others had hoped, but had needed foreign help. Worse still for Mazzini, Italy was a monarchy not a republic and, although the Kingdom was a secular one, Italian life was still overshadowed by the spiritual, if not the temporal, power of the Catholic Church.

Mazzini argued that Italians had had no opportunity to create a new constitution and a new lifestyle. The strong political position of Piedmont in 1860 had enabled Cavour and his successors to force Piedmont's king and constitution on the rest of Italy, along with a liberal government. Mazzini did not quarrel with the exclusion of women as voters or candidates for election – he believed they should stay quietly at home as daughters, wives and mothers to men and have no political or public role. He was, however, concerned that most of the male population, by not being allowed to vote or to stand as candidates, had been excluded from decision-making and had therefore no good reason to support the new state. Democracy (rule by the people) which Mazzini had promised members of 'Young Italy' was as far away as ever. In his view the spirit of the *Risorgimento* was dead, killed by Piedmont's politicians.

b) Historians and the *Risorgimento*

Both Italian and non-Italian historians have over the years developed theories about the importance or otherwise of the *Risorgimento* and have tried to define exactly what it was. Some non-Italians have questioned whether it was ever an actual movement, or was only a ninetenth-century myth created to explain how nationalist ideals of unity and independence were realised.

Suggestions of this kind have not been well received in Italy. The belief in the *Risorgimento* as a revolutionary movement, an active 'resurgence' or 'national rebirth' driven by nationalist ideals of unity and independence, based on a national memory of past glory and the hope of an equally glorious future, is still strong.

Most Italians continue to see it as a movement in which Italy found herself as the result of a long campaign dominated by the larger than life patriotic leaders, Cavour, Garibaldi, Victor Emmanuel II and Mazzini. It is believed that these leaders, with the aid of Napoleon III of France and, acting together, gave Italy unity and independence. Non-Italian historians are much more doubtful about how far, if at all, the *Risorgimento* was important in unifying Italy. They are even more doubtful about whether the 'heroes of the *Risorgimento*' acted together to unite Italy and to give her independence. Ever since G.M.Trevelyan, writing about the *Risorgimento* in the early 1900s, suggested that it was personal hostility and not united action which motivated the 'heroes' and provided 'the mainsprings of action which created a unified state', other British historians have tended to follow a similar line. It has not been a popular theory with Italian historians who have played down 'petty squabbles' and the results of war, and have presented the events of 1860–1 as the great romantic and inevitable climax to a long process of national development and growth which gave Italy back her soul.

Many Italian historians are also philosophers and make use of abstract ideas in teaching about nationalism. This connection between philosophy and history means that much of their historical writing is very hard to follow or, for non-Italians, difficult to understand the reasoning on which it is based. Strong feelings of patriotism are expressed in an emotional and often unclear way. One moderate Italian historian writing in 1943 described the *Risorgimento* as 'a fact or better a process of a spiritual character, an intimate and thorough transformation of national life ... Italy and the *Risorgimento* have both been understood over the centuries, before all else as facts of consciousness, as spiritual attitudes'. In 1960 in a critical review of Dennis Mack Smith's *Italy: A Modern History (1959),* another Italian historian wrote 'the *Risorgimento* was not due to fortunate circumstances or to selfish interests ... it was a spirit of sacrifice, it was suffering in the way of exile and in the galleys, it was the blood of Italian youth on the battlefields ... it was the passion of a people for its Italian identity'. Yet other Italian historians have declared that unification was not brought about by minor disagreements nor by individual action. No mention here of anything as concrete as nationalist movements, secret societies, revolutions, wars or political unification.

British historians are more down-to-earth and their interpretations easier to follow. Dennis Mack Smith, probably the best-known British historian writing about the *Risorgimento*, takes the traditional British line and attributes the creation of a united Italy to the rivalry between Cavour and Garibaldi. It was Piedmontese political ambitions, whether they were those of Cavour or of Garibaldi, which were of supreme importance in deciding what happened in Italy.

The war of 1859 against Austria in the north, described by one historian as 'a carefully planned accident' master-minded by Cavour and Napoleon III, along with Garibaldi's military successes in the south and Cavour's move to stop him reaching Rome, made it possible for Piedmont to force unification on the rest of Italy. After 1860 the *Risorgimento* itself became a part of Italy's shared past and, at this point, some historians suggest, it gradually took on a new identity as a cherished myth, built around a popular quest for national freedom and unity.

Revisionist historians point out that national unity was only one possible result of the Italian struggle for independence. It was not inevitable. They believe that it came about because of French politics and Piedmontese policies, and not from popular nationalist pressure for a unified Italy. This may be so, but the romantic appeal of the *Risorgimento* still persists and seems likely to continue to do so. Its ideals, as we know them, were important because they provided an emotional and political appeal giving Italians a common identity and purpose which fuelled the nationalist cause both before and after unification.

Nationalist movements, secret societies and revolutions did not by themselves 'create' a united Italy – Piedmont did that through a combination of war and politics. However, nationalism did rouse public opinion to support Piedmont's ambitions to lead a unified Italy and to provide its first king and its first national constitution. Without nationalist support a united Italy as early as 1861 would not have been possible.

4 Who United Italy?

Nineteenth-century historians called Cavour 'maker of Italy' but their view is now much less acceptable. Today it seems more likely that he united Italy not so much because he intended to or because he thought it right to do so, but because Garibaldi's unauthorised military successes in southern Italy forced him into action. Dennis Mack Smith and others have dealt in detail with the generally accepted belief of British historians is that it was not the agreements but the disagreements between Cavour and Garibaldi which brought about the unification of Italy by Piedmont.

Stuart Woolf in his *History of Italy 1700–1860*, published in 1979, wrote:

ı The new Italy emerged out of the basic conflict of the opposing patriotic forces (moderate liberals and republican democrats) and the personal hostility of their leaders, not out of what traditional historians were long inclined to interpret as the complementary and harmonious

5 roles of the four 'heroic' leaders – Victor Emmanuel II, Cavour,
   Garibaldi and Mazzini – walking arm in arm towards a unified state.

Woolf mentions here four 'heroes' but there was also a non-Italian,
who cannot be left out of the reckoning, the French Emperor,
Napoleon III.

5 Heroes of the *Risorgimento*

a) Cavour, politician and Garibaldi, soldier

There was indeed hostility as Trevelyan, Mack Smith and Woolf suggest
between Cavour and Garibaldi. How important was it? If Cavour had not
distrusted Garibaldi and feared in 1860 that, after his military successes
in Naples and Sicily, he might make himself permanent ruler of an independent southern Italy and might even turn it into a republic, Cavour
would not have made the decision to invade the Papal States which divided Italy geographically, and so prevented Garibaldi from moving
against Rome. This decision led to an open quarrel between the liberal
Cavour and the radical Garibaldi on the future of the peninsula. It has
been said, with some reason, that Cavour united Italy in order to get the
better of Garibaldi whom he still suspected of being a Mazzini supporter.

Garibaldi for his part disliked Cavour personally and distrusted
diplomacy. He still believed that Italy could only be united by revolutionary means – and that armed action was essential. Like a bull in a
china shop, he had charged into an attack on Sicily and then Naples.
After his unexpected successes there, he planned to go on to take
Venetia and Rome, without considering what the results of this would
have been. Such action would have brought armed intervention by
France to protect her garrison in Rome and probably by Austria to
retain her hold on Venetia. The new and fragile Kingdom of Italy
could not have withstood such a double attack.

It was Cavour's greatest contribution to unification that his
invasion of the the Papal States effectively prevented Garibaldi from
carrying out the second part of his plan, beginning with the attack on
Rome, just as it was Garibaldi's greatest contribution that he was able
to carry out the first part, the conquest of Naples and Sicily, despite
Cavour's opposition.

Garibaldi's willingness to surrender Naples and Sicily to Victor
Emmanuel II avoided civil war and left the way clear for Cavour and
Piedmont to take over Italy. Was this the act of a great and generous
man, laying the spoils of war at the feet of his king, or merely a way of
getting out of a difficult situation, now that the fighting was over?
Historians are divided on this, as on so many questions. However, it
seems probable that both Victor Emmanuel II and Cavour were determined that Garibaldi's contribution was finished and that he should
go, leaving them to continue in a more diplomatic way the process of

unification. With no immediate prospect of further fighting Garibaldi too seems to have been quite happy to return to the simple life on the island of Caprera.

b) Victor Emmanuel II, King of Piedmont and from 1861 also King of Italy

The first king of a united Italy (*Il Re galantuomo*, the gallant King), played little active part in the unification of his new Kingdom. Famous for his incredibly long and deeply cherished moustaches, he was personally popular, with his bluff and hearty manner. Despite his frequently coarse language even Queen Victoria, in whose honour he sacrificed ten centimetres off his moustache, seems to have found him more attractive than she expected when he visited London in 1855:

1 He is so frank, open, just, straightforward, liberal and tolerant, with much sound good sense. He never breaks his word, and you may rely on him; but wild, extravagant, courting adventures and dangers, and with a very strange, short, rough manner ....

Not quite what the French Ambassador had thought about him three years earlier:

1 King Victor Emmanuel is in no sense liberal: his tastes, his education and his whole habit of behaviour all go the other way ... Victor Emmanuel does not like the existing [Piedmontese] constitution, nor does he like parliamentary liberties, nor a free press. He just accepts them tem-
5 porarily as a kind of weapon of war.

Perhaps because it was generally believed that he alone had defied the Austrians and maintained the constitution in 1849, the King has been given a place with the other 'heroes'. Foreign historians have been less enthusistic than Italian ones, being inclined to believe that his only real claim to fame is that he happened to be there at the right time to become the figurehead for Italian nationalists and, after unification, of the new Kingdom of Italy as well. As Garibaldi said, '. . . let Italy be one under *Il Re galantuomo* who is the symbol of our resurgence and the prosperity of our country'. It was who he was and what he represented not what he did, that gave Victor Emmanuel II a special place in Italian history.

c) Mazzini

Mazzini has his place in Woolf's list of heroes but, unlike the others, his active contribution to Italian unification had finished long before 1861. He was the intellectual heart and mind of the movement, quiet and gentle, but not easy to get to know and with few close friends either in Italy or in exile in London. His great moments were in the 1830s and

40s, when his drive for independence and unity were focussed through 'Young Italy' and for a short time made reality by his part in the ill-fated Roman Republic. He was too extreme, too revolutionary and, above all, too republican and anti-Catholic to be acceptable to Piedmontese liberals or to the Church, though he was not without religious beliefs, declaring for instance that God spoke, not through priests because Christianity was now outmoded, but through the people. In exile he kept in touch with what was happening in Italy through the National Society, returning occasionally in secret for short visits, but after 1849 his influence steadily waned and his active part in the *Risorgimento* came to an end. He has always been more admired during his lifetime and after his death by non-Italians than by his fellow countrymen. His voluminous writings in exile – some 10,000 letters and articles filling 100 books – were mostly very mystical and unclear in meaning, and have also always been more often read by foreigners than by Italians.

(For more about Mazzini see pages 98–99 earlier in this chapter and pages 17–21 in Chapter 2.)

d) Napoleon III of France

Napoleon III worried a great deal about what later generations would think of him and in France historians are still divided in their opinions of his aims, ambitions and character. In Britain he has until recently been largely ignored. Whatever his motives for involving himself in Italy, it can be argued that without him and his army the Austrians could not have been driven out of Lombardy in 1859. Piedmont could not have done it alone. An independent and united Italy would have been impossible for many years longer. Many Italians agreed with Garibaldi after the Peace of Villafranca: 'Do not forget the gratitude we owe to Napoleon III and the French army, so many of whose valiant sons have been killed or maimed for the cause of Italy'. Later, after the handing over of Nice, Garibaldi's home town, to the French he was less enthusiastic about Napoleon.

The British historian L.C.B. Seaman is emphatic in his approval: 'Italy must stand for ever in Napoleon's debt for he alone made Italian freedom possible. Without him neither Cavour nor Garibaldi could have united Italy'.

Did Napoleon deserve all this gratitude and applause for his intervention in the affairs of Italy?

By the 1850s Napoleon was alleged to have long been in sympathy with the Italian cause, but had actually done little to help. In fact quite the opposite, because in 1849 he had sent the French army to crush the Roman Republic which they did, remaining afterwards to garrison the city and protect the Pope. At the secret meeting with Cavour at Plombières in July 1858 Napoleon's aim seems to have been not to unite Italy but to keep it divided into a federation of comparatively powerless separate states. As the war of 1859 began

Napoleon proclaimed that his aims were not conquest but ' to restore Italy to the Italians'. He came, he said, in the guise of a liberator as he took command of the Franco-Piedmontese army, but unlike Napoleon I he was no military genius.After the two bloody battles of Magenta and Solferino an armistice was agreed at Villafranca in July as a result of which Austria surrendered Lombardy, via France, to Piedmont but kept Venetia. The war over, Napoleon returned to France. There he found himself the subject of criticism for his conduct of the war. The French were not the only critics. Victor Emmanuel II and Cavour felt Napoleon had betrayed them by going home before he had done what he promised, which was to 'free Italy to the shores of the Adriatic' – in other words, to drive the Austrians out of Venetia as well as Lombardy. Napoleon made some amends in 1866 when as a result of his complicated arrangements with Austria, Prussia and Piedmont he came into possession of Venetia by previous agreement with Austria, and quickly handed it over, again by a prearranged agreement, to the Kingdom of Italy. It did something too to compensate for the handover of Nice and Savoy to France in 1860. Italians were angry too that he refused to withdraw the occupying French troops from Rome until forced to do so by France's war with Prussia in 1870 and the need for reinforcements to defend Paris.

So who did unite Italy? Cavour, Garibaldi, Victor Emmanuel II, Mazzini, or Napoleon III? Was it one of them? Or some of them? Or all of them?

6 The Importance of Piedmont in the Unification of Italy

The new united Italy became a secular constitutional monarchy rather than a republic or federation of states largely because Piedmont itself had remained politically stable as a constitutional monarchy after the failure of the 1848 revolutions. During the 1850s Piedmont developed a strong central government, a well-organised civil service and an effective army, unlike any of the other states. In addition, Piedmont had able political and military leaders in Cavour and Garibaldi, who could use diplomacy and war to best advantage. It also had Mazzini which was both an advantage and a disadvantage.

Piedmont had also acquired a sufficiently good reputation outside Italy to be able to negotiate on a near equal footing with the Great Powers. This reputation had been earned by Cavour's decision to support French and British forces during the Crimean War, a war in which Piedmont had no direct interest, but action which won him a seat among the Great Powers at the Paris peace conference in 1856, and brought him into contact with Napoleon III.

Cavour explained to the Piedmontese parliament his motives for sending troops to the Crimea:

1 Experience of the past years and even centuries has shown how little Italy has benefitted from her revolutions, plots and conspiracies ... I believe that the first condition for the betterment of the state of Italy ... is to raise her reputation ... so that all the nations in the world
5 render justice to her qualities ... it is for our country to show that the sons of Italy can fight with true valour on the fields of glory. I am certain that the laurels our soldiers will win on the battlefields of the east will do more for the future of Italy than all those who have sought to regenerate her with the voice and with the pen.

As well as acquiring international influence Cavour was finding unexpected support within Italy. The Mazzinian National Society which had been a republican and revolutionary movement turned its back on its origins in 1858 and began campaigning instead, in a rather limited way, for Piedmont, arguing that all Italians should rally round Cavour and Victor Emmanuel II as long as Piedmont was ready to work wholeheartedly with the Italian people and to put Italian independence and unity first.

Italian and some other historians have contributed to the view that as Piedmontese leaders had played the major part in the actual process of unification, it was only right that the Kingdom of Italy should have a constitution and civil service as well as a legal and financial system based closely on that of Piedmont.

They backed up this opinion by referring to the correspondence left by Cavour who died suddenly in 1861 from a fever, at the age of 51 and without having had the time, or perhaps the inclination, to write his memoirs. However, he did leave enormous quantities of letters and other papers, both public and personal. These were soon being collected and 'edited' by Piedmontese scholars to give a strongly pro-Piedmontese version of events. The documents were used to illustrate and interpret Piedmont's view of the *Risorgimento* and unification. Where necessary, documents were suppressed or altered or even invented to give Piedmont and Cavour the dominant roles in the unification of Italy. Cavour was shown in a good light and his enemies, whether the Pope, the King of Naples or the republican Mazzini, in a bad one.

British historians writing in the second half of the nineteenth century were deeply influenced by this pro-Piedmontese school of thought, for they found themselves in sympathy with Cavour's moderate liberal politics. At the same time they were attracted to the idea of a war-like yet romantic national hero. Here again Piedmont provided the answer in Garibaldi. If intellectual input was needed Mazzini and his voluminous writings were available.

If primary source material for understanding Cavour's intentions and beliefs was incomplete, inaccurate and had been substantially tampered with, so was that for Garibaldi, but for a different reason. Garibaldi's own account of his motives and exploits were mostly written much later than the events described, and are heavily fictionalised into bad novels. Even his so called *Memoirs* cover only the events up to about 1850, and were substantially 'improved' by other hands before publication. His writings are of very limited value historically in determining his part in events, particularly those important happenings of 1859–61. The new collections of his letters being published in Italy should be more useful as they deal with events which happened at the time of writing.

This chapter began with the words of Massimo D'Azeglio, nobleman, writer, liberal politician, and Prime Minister of Piedmont from 1849 to 1852, who did not die until 1866 and so saw unification almost completed. It seems appropriate to end with another less often quoted remark which shows that he at least was aware of the long and difficult task which lay ahead of the government in 1861. He knew it would take time when he said, 'To make an Italy out of Italians, one must not be in a hurry'. In a country with strong local loyalties people did not automatically become 'Italians' in 1861 or 1866 or 1870 just because they lived in Italy. They remained first and foremost Piedmontese, Neapolitans, Tuscans, Lombards or Venetians. To make Italy into a single nation was going to be a slow process. Unification, so long awaited, was only the first step.

Postscript:

We are left with some important general questions for you to consider and to find your own answers for as we come to the end of the book:

1. Why did unification take so long? In the years from 1815 to 1850 there was unrest and opposition to oppressive absolutist governments. There was resistance, there were secret societies, there was 'Young Italy', and there were revolutions in 1820, 1831–3 and 1848–9 in most of the states.
2. Why did the revolutions all fail to a greater or lesser extent? Look back at Chapter 2 and at your list of reasons why the revolutions failed. What was the most important reason? Even the Roman Republic did not survive but fell to foreign military might. By 1850 very little had been achieved towards Italian unity and independence.
3. How important was foreign involvement – either for good or ill – in the struggle for Italian independence and unity in the years between 1850 and 1861? Consider the parts played by Napoleon III and his French troops, and by Austria.
4. In 1861 the Kingdom of Italy was established. By 1870 unification was complete. Was unification due to individual personalities – 'the heroes' of the *Risorgimento* for instance? Or Napoleon III? Was it the supremacy of Piedmont? Or something else?

References

Lucy Riall, *The Italian Risorgimento*, Routledge 1994.

John Davis and Paul Ginsborg (eds), *Society and Politics in the Age of the Risorgimento* (Cambridge University Press 1991).

L. Seaman, *From Vienna to Versailles* (Methuen, 1955), Chapter 10.

Denis Mack Smith, *Italy, A Modern History* (University of Michigan, 1959).

S.A. Woolf, *History of Italy* (Methuen, 1979).

Vyvyen Brendon, *The Making of Modern Italy 1800–71* (Hodder and Stoughton, 1998).

Summary Diagram

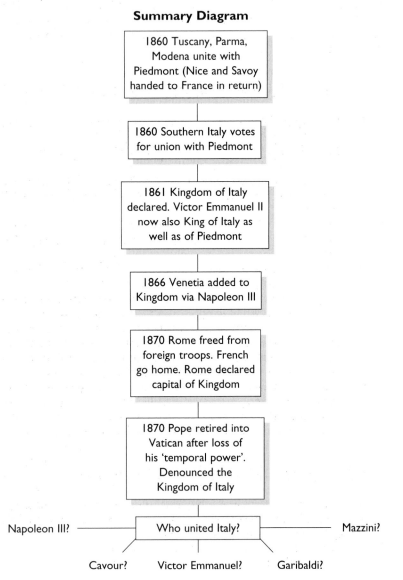

Working on Chapter 6

Firstly Chapter 6 considers the condition of the Italian people during the years between the proclamation of the Kingdom of Italy in 1861 and the events which finally completed the process of unification in 1870. It also provides you with an opportunity to reflect on the contents of the book as a whole and consider again the stages by which Italian independence and unification was won and the significance of the contributions of the men responsible for this achievement. The chapter ends with a historiographical overview of these events – a consideration of the writings of eminent historians who have written about Italian unification.

Answering structured questions based on Chapter 6

1. **(a) (i)** Explain what is meant by 'none were charismatic' (page 94)? (*2 marks*)
        (ii) Explain what is meant by 'The Italy of 1861 was a constitutional monarchy' (page 94)? (*3 marks*)
    b) Why did the Pope threaten to excommunicate Catholics 'who took part in Italian politics or worked for the new secular state'? (*5 marks*)
2. **(a)** During the period 1815–61 in what ways were women 'second class citizens in a macho society'? How did this begin to change after 1861? (*5 marks*)
    (b) In what sense was it true that 'factory work destroyed the family as a self-contained production unit? (*5 marks*)
    (c) Why did the people living in the southern provinces resist the govern-ment's attempts to impose its authority? (*10 marks*)
3. **(a)** Explain what Mazzini meant when he said 'Italy has been put together just as though it were a piece of lifeless mosaic'. (*8 marks*)
    (b) To what extent might it be claimed that Italian unification was brought about in spite of Garibaldi? (*12 marks*)
4. **(a)** Explain the main differences in the views of Italian and non-Italian historians regarding the nature of the *Risorgimento*? (*8 marks*)
    (b) What alternative theories do revisionist historians have about the Italian struggle to achieve independence? (*12 marks*)

Answering essay questions based on Chapter 6

1. 'Italy was free and the states were united politically but they were not united socially or economically'. How valid is this description of Italy during the period 1861–70? (*25 marks*)
2. To what extent did Italian unification depend on the involvement of foreign powers? Explain your answer fully. (*25 marks*)

Further reading

There are a number of helpful books for students wanting to know more about this period of Italian history.

H. Hearder, *Italy in the Age of the Risorgimento 1790–1870* (Longman, 1983)

This very readable book not only deals clearly with political events but provides useful and interesting background reading on literature and the arts, religious issues and economics and social conditions. The chapters on Piedmont and on Cavour are particularly helpful. There is also a section on sources and on the interpretation of the evidence they provide for the unification of Italy.

D. Beales, *The Risorgimento and the Unification of Italy* (Allen and Unwin, 1971; new edition, Longman, 1981)

A short, well-documented book that deals with changing historical views on the *Risorgimento*.

Dennis Mack Smith, *The Making of Italy 1796–1870* (Macmillan, 1968); *Italy: A Modern History* (University of Michigan, 1979)

The author of this book is committed to a particular point of view, that of the historian Mack Smith. *The Making of Italy* tells the story of the *Risorgimento* through documents. *Italy: A Modern History* is another fundamental book on Italian history since 1861.

Professor Stuart J. Woolf, *A History of Italy 1700–1860* (Methuen, 1979)

In this publication the emphasis is mainly on the social history of the period. Included are the findings of Italian social historians.

J.A.S. Grenville, *Europe Reshaped 1848–1878* (Fontana, 1976)

Most general European histories deal very briefly with Italy, but this book is very readable and has a good section on the relations between Cavour and Garibaldi.

New Cambridge Modern History, 1830–1870 Volume X (Cambridge, 1960)

Students who are expecting the highest grades at A Level could look at Chapter 21 of this book.

Biographies make interesting light reading and are well worth a quick skim through. The best biography of Garibaldi is probably still **G.M. Trevelyan's** classic trilogy published over seventy years ago. Written with passion and some degree of bias it provides a good 'easy read'.

J. Ridley, *Garibaldi* (Constable, 1974)

This is a more up-to-date, worthwhile biography.

Denis Mack Smith, *Cavour* (Wiedenfeld and Nicholson, 1985)

This book makes use of much recent research in an up-to-date survey of Cavour's part in the *Risorgimento*. His *Cavour and Garibaldi* (Cambridge, 1954) has been re-issued and is a scholarly comparison of the two men and their policies.

C. Hibbert, *Garibaldi and his Enemies* (Penguin, 1987)

This book is interesting and is worth dipping into to gain a flavour of the period.

W.G. Shreeves, *Nationmaking in Nineteenth Century Europe* (Nelson, 1984)

This has been written specifically for A-Level students and contains extended discussion sections in which some issues are considered in great detail.

L. Riall, *The Italian Risorgimento* (Routledge, 1994)

V. Brendon, *The Making of Italy 1800–71* (Hodder and Stoughton, 1999)

These are two recent recommended texts.

Sources on the Unification of Italy

There is no shortage of published source material in English on this subject.

The best places to start are probably:

D. Beales, *The Risorgimento and the Unification of Italy* (Allen and Unwin, 1971; new edition Longman, 1981)

Dennis Mack Smith, *The Making of Italy 1796–1870* (Macmillan, 1968)

Other helpful publications are:

ed. **N. Gangulee**, *Mazzini's Selected Writings* (Drummond, 1945)

F. Eyck, *Revolutions of 1848–9* (Oliver and Boyd, 1972)

S. Brooks, *Nineteenth Century Europe* (Macmillan, 1983)

G.M. Trevelyan, *Garibaldi's Defence of the Roman Republic* (Longman, 1907)

Sir John Marriot, *Makers of Modern Italy* (OUP, 1943)

For published pictorial sources on nineteenth-century Italian history, see especially:

A. Viotti, *Garibaldi: the Revolutionary and his Men* (Blanford Press, 1979)

For a good range of illustrations on nineteenth-century European history in general, see:

ed. **A. Briggs**, *The Nineteenth Century* (Thames and Hudson, 1970).

Index